Endorsement
Against All Oaas

"With her customary honesty and wit, Kari Paulsen tells a moving story of resilience born out of deep personal faith. This warm and candid spiritual memoir will be read—and loved—by thousands of believers around the globe who are trying to understand the leading of God in their own stories of pain and grace. The writing is as bright and engaging as the author, who skillfully weaves the incidents of an unusually difficult life narrative with compelling insights drawn from years of study and daily Christian experience. Don't miss this book!"

—**Bill Knott,** editor, *Adventist Review* and *Adventist World*

"Once I started reading this remarkable story of human courage and God's faithfulness, I couldn't put it down. Kari's story made me laugh and cry. Read this captivating narrative and you'll discover a life-changing principle: instead of longing for what might have been, you can choose to cut your garment to fit the cloth!"

—**Derek Morris,** author of *Radical Evidence*

"As I've traveled the world, talking to and with my sisters of many different cultures, I find that Christian women have many needs. One need that is outstanding is a need for stories of women of God who have lived through the good and the bad and yet have survived with joy—women with a story to tell of how God has led their lives. They are looking for encouragement. This book by Kari Paulsen is such a book. As I read of her life and the many challenges she faced, but also of her health challenge that has been her "cross" to bear all of her life, and as I look at Kari—quiet, dignified, with a joyful smile, peace on face, and always a listening ear—I know that God lives in her life and lives through her life. I recommend this book to all of my sisters of all cultures and countries. It is a book of what God can do in our lives if we yield ourselves to His control."

—**Heather-Dawn Small,**
Women's Ministries director,
Seventh-day Adventist world church

"What a powerful and moving book! Every girl and woman would be greatly benefited by reading this book! I laughed and cried. Kari's story gives profound advice and courage for dealing with minor or major struggles that life throws our way. It gives the courage to stand for what is right. It gives the insight to understand people of all cultures. The book is hard to put down. Even when not reading it, my mind keeps pondering the stories and profound wisdom it gives. Other than a brief Hello, I do not know Kari. We have never had the opportunity of being together. But I now feel so close to Kari and Jan. I will be eternally grateful for the blessing of this book. My prayer is that everyone will read it. It will be such a blessing to your life!"

—**Janet Page,** associate secretary for Pastoral Spouses and Families, and Prayer, Ministerial Association, Seventh-day Adventist world church

"I deeply admire Kari Paulsen for her profound commitment to ministry, her gracious spirit, and her sharp, witty personality. Her memoir *Against All Odds* provides a poignant and intimate glimpse into this courageous and amazing woman. Her story is a powerful witness of God's grace and a living testimony of the impact of a life of positive choices. What an encouraging and inspiring read!"

—**Kandus Thorp,** vice president, Hope Channel

"As I began reading *Against All Odds,* my interest was captured on the very first page. I could sense the hand of God guiding Kari's life during her childhood days in Norway, with her joys and sorrows in Africa, and in her personal spiritual contacts during the years in England. I was particularly touched with her lifelong commitment to accept any assignment God sent as she stood by her husband Jan's side, ministering so graciously and effectively as the General Conference president's wife.

"In spite of a debilitating disease, Kari persevered. She not only persevered, she persevered graciously without a victim's mentality but with full confidence that God had a divine purpose for her life. Kari's story touched me deeply. She masterfully weaves practical spiritual lessons that apply to each of our lives. The book's frankness and honesty, combined with an unwavering trust in God, is refreshing.

"Every chapter presents a new lesson learned, a new truth discovered, and a new experience gained. I am confident that as you read these pages you will be thrilled as you rediscover the God who is by our side when the odds seem so stacked against us. This is a must-read book that once you start reading you will not want to put down. You will laugh; you will cry; but most of all, you will discover anew the God who is there against all odds."

—**Mark Finley,** evangelist and author

A TRUE STORY

AGAINST
ALL ODDS

A TRUE STORY

AGAINST
ALL ODDS

KARI PAULSEN

Pacific Press®
Publishing Association

Nampa, Idaho | Oshawa, Ontario, Canada
www.pacificpress.com

Cover design by Gerald Lee Monks
Cover design resources supplied by author
Inside design by Aaron Troia

The author assumes full responsiblility for the accuracy of all facts and quotations as cited in this book.

Scripture quotations marked KJV are from the King James Version of the Bible.

Scripture quotations marked NIV are from the HOLY BIBLE, NEW INTER-NATIONAL VERSION®. Copyright © 1973, 1978, 1984, 2011 by Biblica Inc.® Used by permission. All rights reserved worldwide.

Scripture quotations from the *The Message*. Copyright © by Eugene H. Peterson, 1993, 1994, 1995, 1996, 2000, 2001, 2002. Used by permission of NavPress Publishing Group.

You can obtain additional copies of this book by calling toll-free 1-800-765-6955 or by visiting adventistbookcenter.com.

Library of Congress Cataloging-in-Publication Data:

Paulsen, Kari, 1934-
Against all odds : a true story / by Kari Paulsen.
    pages cm
ISBN 13: 978-0-8163-5774-1 (pbk.)
ISBN 10: 0-8163-5774-9 (pbk.)
1. Paulsen, Kari, 1934- 2. Seventh-day Adventists—Norway—Biography.
I. Title.
BX6193.P38A3 2015
286.7092–dc23
[B]

2014049566

February 2015

Contents

Foreword

THE RURAL VALLEY IN EAST Norway where I spent so many of my childhood years is a beautiful place, but I don't like to visit it. The Heddøla River, rich with salmon and trout, flows through neat farmland and thick spruce forests down into the deep waters of lake Heddalsvatnet. Yet whenever I drive along that familiar valley road, or driving south toward Hjuksebø, I always feel a profound sadness settle over me; a feeling that's intensified in autumn when the spruce forests seem to take on some of the brooding darkness of the overcast skies.

In writing this book, I've dredged up many memories that I had long since put to rest, and which perhaps would have been better left undisturbed. The process of reliving some periods in my life hasn't been particularly easy and I've wondered at times if it was really worth doing. But I suppose, as novelist Sir Walter Scott once wrote in his journal, "In literature, as in love, courage is half the battle."

In the end, I decided to tell my story because it's not primarily about me, but about an unlikely course of events that could only have been set in motion by a gracious and powerful Savior.

There are really just two main ideas I hope I can communicate through this narrative.

First, no matter what life has handed you, you can choose, with the Lord's help, to "cut the garment to fit the cloth." You can shape a life that's beautiful and filled with meaning and purpose even amidst less-than-ideal circumstances.

And second, when you're in utter darkness—spiritually or emotionally—you really don't need an awful lot of light to find your way forward. If you can just catch a glimmer of light of the Lord and His salvation and reach out for it, He'll do the rest. I know this is true, because that's what happened to me.

Kari Paulsen
Drammen, Norway
September 2014

Introduction

T HE KITCHEN OF MY CHILDHOOD home in Norway was a magical place. I watched my mother at work at the long table where she carefully undid the seams of old clothing. She would study the fabric, holding it up and turning it this way and that, considering what new garment she could make. A new pinafore for my sister or me. A new coat to help ward off the chill of sub-zero arctic winters. Having made her decision, she'd lay the fabric out on the table and begin cutting out shapes with quick snips of her dressmakers' scissors. Soon, I'd hear the rhythmic hum of her hand-powered Singer sewing machine as she began to transform a long-discarded dress or coat into new, smart clothes for her family.

It was the early 1940s, the first turbulent years of World War II. Our family's home was located in a quiet valley of East Norway, just five kilometers from the small town of Notodden. Our valley was usually a tranquil, rural area, yet this isolated place played a major part in one of the most dramatic affairs of the war—the race between Hitler and the Allies to produce an atomic bomb.

At the center of the drama was a mysterious substance known as "heavy water," which scientists both in Germany and Great Britain realized was an essential piece of the puzzle in producing atomic energy. This "heavy water" helps transform common uranium into weapons-grade plutonium. When war broke out in Europe, Norway was the only country in the world with a commercial heavy-water plant. The main factory was Vemork, a hydroelectric power plant outside Rjukan—located about seventy-five kilometers from where we lived. But Notodden, our closest town just three miles away, also housed a power station where scientists connected with heavy water production worked.

I can still hear the sounds of the Allied planes flying overhead at night. The whole community was pitched in darkness, with every window covered by heavy black roller blinds. There was the lighter, quicker *thrum, thum, thrum* of the smaller fighter planes—I didn't mind *that* sound too much. But the bombers . . . I can still almost feel the deep, resonant, drumming vibrations of those heavy planes as they passed over our house, headed toward the Norsk Hydro heavy water production plants. We would wait and listen . . . Would they strike Notodden tonight?

Our nearness to these power plants meant that the Norwegian resistance was active in the region. The railway line ran past our property just a few hundred meters away down a steep embankment—it took just a couple of minutes for us children to slide down the slope from our home to the railway station.

The heavy water was transported by train, and so sometimes at night the Norwegian resistance would detonate explosives on the railway tracks near our house, bringing a swarm of German soldiers to search nearby farms. The soldiers would go from room to room in our house, moving furniture aside, pulling down pictures from the wall, and thrusting their bayonets into any space they deemed large enough to harbor a man. I still shiver when I remember how one solider drove his bayonet down into a large antique rose-painted *kiste*—or chest—where Mother kept spare blankets and linens. I knew there was no one hiding inside, but for a child with an overactive imagination, just the sight of that blade being plunged down so forcefully through the blankets was horrifying. What if there *had* been someone crouched inside?

A sense of anxiety had invaded old relationships in our community. Longtime neighbors began to look warily at each other, wondering who was sympathetic with our Nazi occupiers and who was a member of the resistance. Who would report forbidden radios, tuned to the BBC war bulletins? Who could be trusted?

Introduction

On the wall of the small, one-room schoolhouse I attended, there was a large map of Norway. We children knew, however, that the teacher had pinned underneath the map a photo of exiled Norwegian King Haakon VII. Our teacher was a kind man and a good teacher—someone who cared deeply for the students in his charge. Yet this did not save him when two students, whose parents were Nazi sympathizers, told local authorities about the forbidden picture behind the map. Our teacher was sent to a prison camp in the north, far up above the Arctic Circle, where he suffered dreadful hardship for the duration of the war. But at least he survived.

In some ways, everyday life during the occupation continued as normal: the seasons came and went; our parents continued with their work; we children went to school—although after our teacher was taken away, we relied on a succession of substitute teachers and often the school was closed. Yet, it wasn't long before each day became a struggle to find the basics of life. Yes, we had coupons for food rations and clothes—but our coupons only had value if there was food on the shelves or clothes and shoes to buy, and too often the shelves were empty. If we needed medicine, there was often none to be had. If we children grew out of our clothes, or if we wore holes in our coats and shoes, there was nowhere to buy replacements, even if we did have coupons.

And so, sitting at our kitchen table, my mother continued to weave her magic on old garments. There's no doubt she was a skilled seamstress, but in hindsight I realize that her most important gift was her imagination. She had an amazing ability to look beyond worn fabric and outdated styles; she would hold up an old shirt or dress to the light and see the potential for something new and fresh.

It has been more than seventy years since I watched my mother sitting in front of her old black Singer machine, but I can still see her clearly in my memory. Since then, my life has taken me on a path that I could never, in a million years, have predicted. It has taken me a long way from that quiet Norwegian valley, from a family life filled with tensions and unhappiness, where religion played no meaningful role beyond the expected christenings and confirmations.

Instead, life took me on an adventure—from Africa, to Europe, to the United States—where Christ walked alongside me, through both adversities and joys. In recent years, especially, as wife of the president of the Seventh-day Adventist world church, I had a front-seat perspective on how the Lord is leading us, His people, in extraordinary ways around the world today.

Yet along with adventure, life has also handed me a few "gifts" that I could happily have done without. There have been challenges and some heartbreaks, as well as a life-changing illness that for the past forty years has shadowed me each day and kept me from doing many things I would have loved to do.

I've written this book because I've come to recognize the powerful gift that my mother gave me all those years ago as she pulled apart the seams of old clothes and laid the fabric flat on her kitchen table. No matter what old, discarded material lay in front of her, she looked at it and saw the beauty she could create. She demonstrated over and over again the truth of an old European proverb, "You must cut the garment to fit the cloth." In other words, you have to work with what you've got. You have no choice! It's no use lamenting what you wish you had—whatever life hands you, you have the opportunity to take it and fashion it into something meaningful.

If you're like me, your life probably doesn't look perfect. You may have worries about your children or finances, or you may not have the job you wish you had, or you or a loved one may be dealing with discouraging health news.

You can't wish challenges away, but I've learned—often the hard way—that you can choose every day to "cut the garment to fit the cloth"; to work with the circumstances you have—whether they're good, bad, or indifferent. Try holding the fabric of your life up to the light, and turn it this way and that. Look closely at the material and try to see past the worn places. Study the fabric itself and search for its original beauty. Are there possibilities there? With the Lord by your side, could you reshape it a little, perhaps trim it here or there, and make something new? Something beautiful?

Chapter 1

At Journey's Start

THERE'S AN IMAGE FROM MY childhood that's imprinted on my mind. It's a mental "snapshot" of a particular moment in time that I always carry with me. In the center of the picture is a lake, with bright winter sunshine glistening on its snowy surface. The lake is surrounded by tall mountains covered with gleaming white snow that's too bright for eyes to linger on for long. The evergreens around the lake and beside the railway tracks also carry a frosting of white, and to the left I can glimpse some of the snow-covered roofs of houses.

I am eleven years old and I'm sitting on the train with my father, listening to the low chugging of the train's steam engines as it idles at the station. I'm staring at the scene out my window, and repeating to myself, *Kari, don't forget this. Remember every detail. Don't forget how beautiful this is.*

I've just said goodbye to my mother on the station platform, and she did something that surprised and unsettled me; something that almost never happened in our family. She bent down, gathered me into her arms, and hugged me.

It's definitely not a good sign, I tell myself.

Then the train engines grow louder and quicken and the beautiful, snowy image in front of me begins to grow smaller and smaller as the train pulls away from the station.

Through the hours, as the train heads along the tracks toward Oslo, I keep my head turned toward the window, but I see little of the changing landscape outside. Instead, I see a sunshine-dappled scene of snow, lake, trees, village, and mountains. The beautiful, familiar backdrop of my childhood.

I fully expect I've seen it for the last time.

"You're going to die!"

It was four years earlier, during a silly argument with my older brother and some neighborhood children—I don't even remember now what it was about—that I discovered I didn't have long left to live. I was seven years old and my brother, sister, and friends had always been physically stronger than me. But I wasn't completely defenseless in these childhood scraps; my weapon of choice was my "word power" and I often deployed it to great effect. Yet on this particular day, I must have especially infuriated them because they shot back with a piece of information that shattered my world.

"You're going to die!" they told me.

"Well, of course," I said. "Everyone has to die sometime."

"No, no," they said. "You're going to die soon. There's something wrong with your heart and you could just drop dead at any time. Maybe tomorrow, or even today!

"But don't tell your mother and father we told you, because you're not supposed to know," they said. "We heard them talking about it and we know it's true!"

I was stunned. It was too much to take in, and yet I had no reason to disbelieve them—it explained so much: the doctor's visits, the hushed conversations between my parents, the trouble I had keeping up with the other kids as they ran and played in the schoolyard. And yet, it had never, ever crossed my mind that all these things meant I was going to die soon.

For once, I had no words to offer the other children—no smart comebacks. I turned and ran to the barn where I buried myself in the sweet-smelling hay and began to cry and cry.

If the knowledge of my imminent death didn't fully sink in then, it certainly did a little over a year later as our small school planned its year-end program. Grades one to three were to perform a play about colors with the girls dressed in crepe paper dresses and the boys in capes. In my memory, I can still hear the rustle of the crepe paper as we moved around in our assigned positions and to my ears it was a frightening, ominous sound.

I had been cast to represent death and I was dressed in black. (In hindsight, I can only wonder what my beloved teacher was thinking, given his knowledge of my illness and prognosis.) I can remember my feelings as clearly as if it happened just yesterday. I stood there, clad in my somber costume, lost and alone. *Nobody can save me*, I thought. And then I had to speak the lines I'd been given.

"Døden er kold og sort,
Kaller for evig bort."
Or, *"Death is cold and black,*
Forever calling us back."

My sister was dressed in green—her verse was about hope. I wished so much that my dress was green, too, and that no one had to wear black.

It's an overwhelming, confusing experience for a little girl to contemplate death. What did it really mean? I had no clear understanding. Sometimes during the summer, I'd gone with my mother to the churchyard to tend the graves of family members. We'd plant and water flowers, do some weeding, and make everything look nice and tidy. And then when we were finished, we'd sit down to rest on the slabs of marble.

How cold these grave stones are, I'd often thought. *And how heavy they are. How dark it must be inside those graves.*

And now I knew that I'd soon be in there, too, in the dark and the cold. I'd always suffered with terrible claustrophobia and this added to my nightmare. They'd bury me in the ground and I'd be trapped underneath one of those heavy, heavy stones.

I was just a baby when my mother began to suspect I wasn't as robust as I should have been—her intuition told her that something wasn't quite right. She took me to the local doctor who looked me over and said confidently, "Oh, she's just fine. You'll see. She's a bit weak now but she'll grow stronger."

But I didn't. My stamina continued to lag behind that of other children my age and so when I was three, the doctor decided to take out my tonsils and adenoids. "That'll help her," he said. But it made no difference at all.

A severe bout of whooping cough when I was seven years old made me very ill and our country doctor finally decided he needed some backup. He sent me to what was then known as a "heart and lung specialist" and I underwent a vast array of X-rays, blood tests, and examinations.

When my mother and I went back for the results, the doctor told me to go out into the waiting room and I sat there for what seemed like a very long time. Later, I learned what he'd told my mother that day.

"Yes," he said, "your daughter has had a very bad case of whooping cough. But that's not the real problem. Kari has a heart defect and it means she probably won't survive her teen years. You need to be careful how you treat her. If she gets a sudden fright, she could die. Be careful how you discipline her—no spanking and don't let her get frightened. And whatever you do, don't tell her about her heart problem. She must be kept as calm as possible."

Daring to hope

Norway in 1945 was a country that was in turmoil, still trying to grapple with the tremendous destruction and privations of the war years. The German occupation of Norway had begun on April 9, 1940, when Hitler's *Operation Weserübung* saw some ten thousand German soldiers attack by both sea and air. In the days that followed, the Norwegian government—including the royal family—managed to escape to London to begin doing what they could to organize a resistance movement. But for three million ordinary Norwegians left behind, the occupation marked the start of five long years of censorship, food shortages, and a constant struggle to find adequate clothes, shoes, and other basic necessities. And then there was, of course, an ever-present sense of fear and uncertainty as the war in Europe ground on relentlessly.

Liberation for Norway finally came on May 8, 1945, when German forces surrendered and members of the Norwegian resistance movement occupied the Royal Palace in Oslo. However, the joy of the moment soon gave way to a realization that the daunting task of rebuilding our nation lay ahead.

The war that had devastated so much of Europe had left tremendous scars on Norway. An estimated ten thousand citizens had been killed, directly or indirectly, because of the war and many had suffered terribly in prison camps. Others, especially political activists, Jews, intellectuals, and many professionals, had fled Norway early in the war and had spent the ensuing years as refugees. The nation's economy was utterly ruined—Norway's production capacity was effectively halved by German management, which was concerned only with funneling raw resources to the Nazi war machine.

Every town and village in Norway also bore deep psychological wounds from the occupation and there was a national debate about how to deal with the traitors among us; those men and women who had collaborated with the occupiers.

This was the turbulent setting in which my mother and father set out to find the best medical care they could for their young daughter and her damaged heart. My father had two sisters living in Oslo and one of them was friends with the CEO of the Oslo University Hospital. During the German occupation, many of the hospital staff had fled to Sweden, which was neutral. The summer of 1945 saw a good number of them returning to the city and to their old posts at the hospital, and among them was a promising young surgeon named Dr. Carl Semb.

My mother contacted the doctor who had diagnosed my heart condition and asked him for a referral to this surgeon at Oslo University Hospital. He refused point blank. "No," he said, "there's no point." And as far as he was concerned, that was that.

But my aunt, who lived in Oslo, had a good measure of our family's trademark determination. She heard from her friend, the University Hospital CEO, that Dr. Semb was returning to Norway and that he wanted to start a heart surgery program at the hospital. My aunt told my parents, "Bring Kari to the city. We'll sort it out once she's here."

So in the summer of 1945, I traveled to Oslo, encouraged by a promise that if I went, my aunt would take me to visit the British and American warships that were anchored in the city's harbor, and that I'd also get to see the Norwegian royal family return from their wartime exile in London.

She kept her word, and I had a wonderful time. On one of the American ships, I was given a glass of dark, bubbly liquid, which a soldier informed me was a delicious new drink called "Coca-Cola." I took a big sip and almost spat it straight out again—it was simply *awful*—but I drank it to the last drop, scared of offending my kind hosts.

King Haakon and his family returned home to Norway aboard the cruiser HMS *Norfolk* on June 7, and it was a day I will never forget. My aunt took me to the waterfront to join the huge crowds of cheering people. There was a palpable sense that now, finally, our nation could begin to heal from its five-year ordeal of Nazi occupation.

A small victory

I was admitted to the University Hospital as a private patient and placed in the adult ward to keep me away from the viruses and germs of the children's ward. For a ten-year-old who had seen little of the world, my summer in the hospital was a frightening time. In the bed next to me there was an actress, also named Kari, and she always spoke kindly to me and sometimes explained things I didn't understand.

One day, a man in a wheelchair was wheeled into the hallway next to our ward. Looking back now, I realize he was probably around forty years old, yet at the time he seemed very old. He was gaunt and he sat without moving, but his eyes were like those of a wild animal. It was his hands, however, with their strangely elongated fingers that drew and held my horrified eyes. He was like a living scarecrow.

My friend, Kari, in the next bed said to me, "Don't worry about it.

He has lost his mind, but he's a hero—he's done a very good thing."
She told me that he'd been a resistance fighter who had been arrested
and tortured by the Gestapo in an effort to extract the names of other
members of his underground cell. They'd pulled every joint of his
hands and feet, and yet he hadn't betrayed his friends.

I had nightmares for a long time afterward.

There was another person who loomed large during my time at
the hospital—the ward matron. She was a humorless, bad-tempered
woman who terrorized nurses and patients alike, and my association
with her got off to a very poor start.

One of the other nurses had taken a liking to me and sometimes,
when the matron was occupied elsewhere, she allowed me into the
office where I sat at the matron's big wooden desk and enjoyed
pecking away, one-fingered, at the keys of the matron's typewriter.

One day, as I sat happily typing away, there was a commotion up
one end of the corridor and it became quickly apparent that the
matron was returning to her office sooner than expected. I quickly
ducked underneath the desk into the knee hole and pushed myself
as far back against the wall as I could. The matron came into the
room, sat down at her desk, and began chastising her secretary for
no apparent reason.

I've never been noted for my meekness in the face of injustice
or insult and so I did what, at the time, seemed entirely reasonable.
I bit the matron's leg. And thus began a relationship that added an
extra layer of interest to my time at the Oslo University Hospital.

This was a teaching hospital and so I was often made to feel like
an exhibit in a museum. The doctor would come on his morning
rounds, trailed by an assortment of students and young doctors.
After a perfunctory greeting, he would begin his examination, explaining my condition and treatment for the benefit of his audience.

Sometimes I was summoned to a lecture room in the hospital
and displayed up front before a room filled with some sixty to eighty
students. I can still hear the droning voice of the professor as he began his lecture. "Now this is Kari, and her heart sounds something
like the machines in Manchester. . . ."

One day the matron prepared me for my lecture room appearance and to punish me for my various misdemeanors, she dressed me in some old-fashioned women's underwear—the type that wrapped right around me. I must have looked a sight—a skinny ten-year-old girl in oversized ladies underwear. When the professor removed the sheet and began his talk, the students burst into loud laughter. I was humiliated.

The next day the matron informed me that my presence would again be required in the lecture room. As soon as I was alone, I got down out of my bed and climbed up one flight of stairs to the ninth floor of the hospital to the entrance of the children's ward. The perfect camouflage! I blended right in and no one twigged to the fact that I shouldn't have been there. I sat there for hours as staff searched the hospital for their missing patient. When I was sure the lecture was over, I came back down the stairs, and received a long, angry lecture from the matron.

"Well, I'll do it again," I said defiantly. "And I'll keep doing it for as long as you dress me in that ugly underwear."

She never did it again, and I savored the episode as a victory.

A guinea pig

At the end of the summer, the hospital sent word to my parents that Dr. Semb would like to operate on me. I would be the first person in Norway to have heart surgery of any kind and in the letter to my parents the doctors gave me a 50/50 chance of survival.

"However, if you don't let us at least try to operate, it's very doubtful she'll survive puberty," they said.

I went back home while my parents wrestled with this decision and finally, right before Christmas, they told me that I'd be returning to Oslo in the New Year to have the operation.

With the devastating "honesty" of children, my brother, sister, and our playmates informed me I was being sent back to Oslo to be a guinea pig. I had no clue what it meant to be guinea pig, but they told me, "This is when doctors don't know what to do. They'll cut you open, look at your heart, and figure out how to fix it. You'll probably die, but at least they'll know what to do with the next person!"

I had little interest in being a guinea pig—no matter how useful that may be to medical science—but I had no choice. Eleven-year-olds have little say in their own fate. I remember, though, how worried I was in the days before I left my home for what I firmly believed would be the last time.

A younger sister had recently been born into our family—my replacement, I thought—and my mother couldn't come with me to the hospital, so it fell to my father to take me. We left on January 2, 1946, and it was on this day that I sat on the train and fixed in my mind an image of beauty I hoped would stay with me when I was dead.

Today, I can still see the sunny winter scene clearly in my mind's eye. The spruce trees, the mountains, the lake, the blankets of snow. Every time I recall the image to my mind, it brings with it a whole load of emotions.

I was a fearful eleven-year-old girl, who was being carried—so I thought at the time—inexorably toward my death. Yet if I could but have known it, that train trip to Oslo was actually just the beginning of my life's journey—an adventure-filled trip that has already lasted more than seven decades.

I also had no idea that this first stop on my journey would lead me to a completely unexpected encounter with a Divine Friend—One who would travel with me the rest of the way.

Chapter 2
A Life-Changing Promise

P AIN, WHETHER PHYSICAL OR EMOTIONAL, is an intensely isolating experience. You can't hand it off to someone else when you need a break, there's no "pause button" you can hit; severe pain is all-enveloping, all-consuming. At its worst, pain can demonstrate the limits of language to describe human experience. Pain falls into two broad categories, says *New York Times* journalist Dana Jennings, writing about his experience with prostate cancer, "the kind you can articulate, and the pain that is beyond words."*

I have little patience for those who suggest that the experience of pain is somehow ennobling or poetic and I've found that philosophical clichés provide little comfort when you're actually suffering. Friedrich Nietzsche's idea, "That which does not kill us makes us stronger," is perhaps a nice-sounding slogan but rings empty for someone struggling with a heavy psychological or physical burden.

Of course, the experience of pain is common to us all—no one escapes it—and I suppose on this level it's a "humanizing" experience, something that hopefully teaches us a bit about humility, empathy, and our essential sameness, regardless of race, gender, background, or education.

Yet when we're caught in the grip of a "pain beyond words," there's little room for philosophizing. Sometimes, the best we can hope for is to simply endure.

---

* Dana Jennings, "Pain Beyond Words, and an Impulse Just to Endure," *New York Times*, September 21, 2009.

A Life-Changing Promise

"Just a small operation"

My second visit to Oslo University Hospital was overlaid with a sense of dread. I was admitted first to the medical ward for a week for some final tests before the operation to attempt to repair my heart defect.

An internist named Professor Mueller came to visit me on the final day of my stay in the medical ward, trailed by his ever-present entourage of trainees and students.

"Hello, Kari," he said. "Tomorrow you will be transferred to ward three—the surgical ward. You'll have a small operation and afterward you'll feel just fine."

I'd overheard enough about my condition to know when an adult wasn't being entirely straightforward with me. So I looked the doctor straight in the eye and said in my broad rural dialect, "Do you know what? You'll never go to heaven because you're lying."

He didn't say another word. He just looked at me and walked away.

The next day a nurse took me in a wheelchair over to ward three, then took me to the operating theater so I could see what it was going to be like.

My surgery had the distinction of being the first heart surgery ever performed in Norway, although it was a distinction I could happily have done without. Perhaps one of the biggest challenges for the hospital was the lack of experienced theater staff to assist Dr. Semb, who would be performing the surgery. Later, a nurse confided to me that some of the less-experienced nurses had speculated about things that could go wrong, imagining blood from my heart spurting up uncontrollably like a geyser when the surgeon opened me up.

Interest in the procedure was understandably high and the hospital staff had set up scaffolding with extra seating around the edges of the operating room to accommodate the doctors and medical students who would be coming to observe. As the nurse wheeled me through the cold, sterile room, I looked around me with fear.

The nurses were kind and assured me, "It's just a small operation, and you'll feel so much better afterward." Yet I wasn't reassured.

Why do adults so often underestimate a child's capacity to interpret what's really happening around them?

I remember my pre-operation visit to the operating theater, but then I remember nothing more until about a week later.

Pain and penicillin

The first image that seeped through my unconsciousness was the image of the lake and snow-covered mountains that I had worked so intensely to emblazon on my mind. But something was wrong—I felt like the mountain was sitting on top of my chest.

"Please, can't you take this mountain off me?" I begged the nurses. The surgeon had removed one of my ribs and I felt like I couldn't draw breath. And the pain . . . It was unspeakable. In those days, children were not given heavy painkillers and so I lay there, gripped by agony, gasping for air. I couldn't move; I was in and out of consciousness. I wanted to die.

It wasn't a transitory thought. I truly wanted to die. Being alive meant experiencing a torture I hadn't even imagined could exist. But I lived.

These early days of my recovery were complicated by the fact that blood transfusions at the time were still relatively primitive. Medical science hadn't yet discovered the vital differences between positive and negative blood types. My blood type is AB negative, yet I was given transfusions of both positive and negative blood, making me a very sick little girl, indeed.

Another problem was the fluid that kept collecting around my lungs. When this began to interfere too much with my breathing, two orderlies held me sitting up on my bed while a doctor inserted a needle through my back into each of the plural spaces around my lungs and suctioned out the fluid. Each time the doctor drew back on the needle, both fluid and air was sucked out of my chest. The pain was almost more than I could bear, but I couldn't even find the air to scream.

My physical pain was compounded by my sense that I was alone. My father had had more than enough early on, and he'd taken the train back home again on the day of my surgery. This was an era in which children were kept in the dark about both their condition and their treatment. No doctor explained what he was doing or why. Some nurses were kind, but not one would tell me what was happening to me.

Of course, I'd absorbed quite a lot of information about my condition by listening to medical staff talk to each other and by sneaking peeks at my chart whenever I had the opportunity. But whenever I asked a direct question, it was brushed aside.

Who could I trust to tell me the truth? There was no one, and I felt utterly abandoned.

I was placed in a room with a woman who was also recovering from a surgery, and I could hear her cursing as waves of pain hit her. A nurse came into the room and said to her, "If you fuss and carry on, you'll just feel even more ill." She pointed to me in the next bed and said, "Look at this child here—she doesn't get anything like you're getting for her pain, and yet she stays quiet. You should learn from her." That lesson has stayed with me through the years— sometimes in the face of overwhelming pain or difficulty, your best strategy is simply to quiet yourself and not waste strength railing against something you cannot change.

As I lay there, I sometimes experienced an intense thirst and I dreamed of a glass of the cold, refreshing drink my mother brewed at home from honeysuckle and other ingredients. We drank this drink during the summer and on special occasions and although the alcohol content was probably negligible, our family called it "beer."

In my semi-conscious state, as my throat burned for something cool and soothing, I kept calling out, "Please, won't someone bring me some of my mother's beer?"

"Well, can you believe that?" I heard one nurse say to another. "Can you imagine what sort of home this little girl comes from?" I was incensed, but was in no position to protest.

I was fortunate that my case had generated quite a stir in the hospital where all surgeries, apart from emergencies, had been canceled on the day of my surgery. There happened to be some American soldiers at the University Hospital who heard about the little girl who'd survived a risky heart repair operation and was now struggling to recover from a post-operative infection. I don't know how they did it, and I don't even know their names, but these soldiers arranged for me to receive access to penicillin—a drug that was reserved for American military use only and which was out of reach for Norway's civilian population. A nurse told me later that the precious medicine had arrived from America on a U. S. military plane.

I was given a two-week course of penicillin injections. The medicine was a thick, viscous fluid that had to be injected every three hours, day and night, with a heavy gauge needle. Every injection burned like fire. For a child who was just skin and bone, finding a new place to inject each time was also a challenge. It was so painful—and I begged the nurses not to do it—but those injections saved my life.

These soldiers also sent me a beautiful big box filled with all sorts of things that wartime rationing had made impossible to get— foods like nuts, oranges, dates, figs, and bananas. They also gave me a pink dress and a pair of brown patent leather shoes. The shoes were a size too small, but they were the most beautiful shoes I'd ever seen, and so later on I stubbornly wore them—painfully but with pride. At the time, I was too sick to even acknowledge these soldiers' generosity and I've always regretted not being able to thank them.

A promise

Toward the end of the course of penicillin, I started to feel just a little bit better and I began to think that perhaps living wouldn't be so bad.

It was then that I had a life-altering conversation with the Unknown Person "up there." As I lay in my bed, with the familiar sounds of the ward around me, I said to Him, "If You let me get through this, I'll become a Christian."

My recovery continued, long and painful but steady. In the weeks and months that followed, my sense of resolve never wavered. I'd made a bargain with the Almighty; He seemed to be keeping His side of it and I intended to keep mine.

I may have been determined but there was one overwhelming obstacle before me. I wondered, *How exactly does one go about becoming a Christian?* I had no idea.

Even though Norway was—and still is—considered a Christian nation, my confusion was perhaps quite natural. The *Den norske kyrkja,* the Church of Norway, is the state church and has been, more or less, since 1537 when King Christian III of Denmark and Norway declared Lutheranism the official religion of the nation.

The practice of Lutheranism is ingrained within Norway's culture; it's as Norwegian as fjords and salmon. Most Norwegians are registered at baptism as members of the church and many of them simply don't bother to change their status, regardless of their religious practice or lack thereof. Many are baptized, confirmed, married, and buried within the rites of the church, yet have next to no understanding about the practice of Christianity.

So, of course, I'd been christened in the Church of Norway as a baby, and I knew I'd go through the confirmation process when I approached thirteen years of age. Yet no one had ever explained to me what it meant to be a *Christian,* as opposed to simply being a member of the Lutheran Church. And to my mind, these two things weren't necessarily the same thing.

I continued to recover and to ponder my dilemma and after what seemed like a very long time, I was finally sent back home.

Chapter 3
The Search Begins

S TUBBORN" WAS A DESCRIPTION OF myself I heard many times during my childhood and teen years and it was probably quite accurate. It's also a label that my husband of more than five decades still sometimes applies to me, although in his case I know—or at least, I hope—it's mostly used with affection.

Being stubborn is a characteristic that has stood me in good stead through the years, but I know sometimes those close to me haven't always seen it in positive terms. We call people "stubborn" when they infuriate us with their apparent inflexibility, or when they refuse to see the "correct" (which actually means "our") point of view.

To my mind, though, being stubborn has gained an unfairly negative connation. I suspect that if I hadn't been born stubborn—if my nature had been more compliant and passive—I may not have lived long enough to see much past adolescence, let alone deal with the various life-bumps I've experienced in the decades since.

Stubborn? Yes, I'm happy to claim this label but perhaps we could reframe it slightly. I think being "stubborn" is more about *knowing yourself*. It's about understanding and articulating what's most important to you—people, principles, ideas, goals—and letting these things guide your path, no matter how circumstances buffet you.

My struggle to recover from heart surgery was perhaps the first big test of my stubborn nature. Now as an eleven-year-old, looking toward a future I never thought I'd see, the next great test loomed. How was I going to be able to make good on my bargain with God and become a real Christian?

The Search Begins

Home again

With my return home from the hospital in the spring of 1946, I began the slow process of building up my strength and returning to the everyday routines of life: school, chores, playing with friends. Our family schedule, however, didn't include church attendance.

My parents were good, law-abiding citizens but they simply weren't in a position to help me in my quest to become a believing, practicing Christian. They fell into the category of "non-Christian Lutherans," as they were known—those who entered church only to be christened, confirmed, and married.

Complicating my home life was the constant atmosphere of conflict that seemed to permeate our day-to-day activities. Looking back, I've come to see that, individually, my mother and father were good people, but together they were dysfunctional. They came from vastly different backgrounds—my father was the son of a former landowning family that had fallen on hard times, but which had retained its pride and cultured way of life. My mother was from a humbler farming family.

My father, a tall, good-looking man, was fiercely proud, reserved, and very intelligent. But he was moody and often out of sorts. His temper was legendary, and we children learned to move quickly out of his way when he was angry.

My mother, on the other hand, had an incredible capacity for happiness and fun. It seemed that she brightened any room, and any occasion, simply through the sheer force of her good humor and imagination. I learned a lot from her about how to extract as much joy as possible out of any situation.

But together, my mother and father were a disaster; they fought long and loudly and sometimes their arguments turned violent. It's difficult for children growing up in a home where their parents fight. There is an ever-present sense of dread; the fear of not knowing exactly what will spark a bad mood that may flare into something more frightening.

The discord in our home was isolating for my siblings and me. We couldn't invite our friends to our home—we knew the atmosphere could turn ugly very quickly—and so we felt shy about accepting invitations to our friends' homes, knowing we couldn't reciprocate.

To a certain extent, I learned how to "float above" some of the unpleasantness. Perhaps it was the fact that I escaped much of the physical punishment because of my heart defect, or because I was so often ill in bed, or maybe because I took every opportunity I could to get out of the house for stays with my grandparents or other relatives. Sometimes I felt as if I was a mere bystander, a stranger in our family, and I would analyze the situation through objective, dispassionate eyes. I suspect now this was a mechanism I developed to protect myself from being emotionally damaged by what was happening around me.

I also learned that, unlike my siblings, I could sometimes stop a precarious situation from spiraling out of control if I confronted my father. My heart condition meant that he wouldn't dare hit me, and perhaps that knowledge made me more assertive. Tragically, my brother had no such shield and he bore much of my father's violence.

So, I felt there was little I could gain from my family in my mission to become a real Christian—we simply didn't talk about things like that.

Too many questions

I had been taught the Lord's Prayer in school and we'd also learned a grace to sing or say before meals. I thought, *Maybe I should just say the Lord's Prayer when I go to bed at night.* More often than not, though, I would fall asleep before I got through it. And as for the grace, it would be too embarrassing to sit at the table saying a long prayer before meals as the rest of my family just dived in. I didn't want to draw attention to myself.

As time passed, I began to grow nervous. *Whoever is up there is going to strike me dead if I don't do what I promised,* I thought. *There's a lightning bolt somewhere with my name on it.*

When I turned thirteen, I began attending confirmation classes. Each week we learned hymns, Bible verses, and of course, the

Lutheran catechism. I was also given a Bible, so I began to read it at home, starting in Genesis. It was a book, so naturally I thought it best to simply start on the first page and read it through. I got to Exodus and was surprised to notice there were differences between the Ten Commandments recorded in the Bible and those we were learning from the catechism.

This is strange, I thought. *The catechism just says to remember the "rest day" to keep it holy, but here in the Bible there's all this rigmarole about the seventh day.*

At the next confirmation class, I raised my hand and asked the minister about the discrepancy.

"Well, it's because our Lord was raised on the Sunday—that's why we keep this day holy," he said.

"Oh, I see. So the Bible tells us that the rest day became Sunday," I said.

"Well, no," he said. "It's not actually written in the Bible, but it was such an important happening, Jesus rising from the dead, and so that's why we worship on Sunday."

I didn't find the minister's explanation 100 percent convincing, but I put it aside for a while.

I continued reading through the Bible until I was defeated by the "begats" and I began to think that perhaps the Old Testament was too complicated for a thirteen-year-old. I flipped over to the New Testament and began reading, and there I discovered some fodder for more questions.

I raised my hand at the next confirmation class. "Why is it that Jesus wasn't christened and He wasn't confirmed? And why was He baptized when He was old by being dipped in a river?"

The minister had learned his lesson. "Kari, you ask far too many questions," he said. "The ministers of our church have studied Latin, Greek, and Hebrew and they aren't troubled by these things, so I think you can probably stop worrying."

I wasn't at all happy with his answer. Why shouldn't I understand it? I continued with the confirmation classes, but I knew deep inside that I really wasn't becoming a Christian.

Against All Odds

On the Sunday of our confirmation, all the boys and girls from my class were expected to take first communion.

To my mind, taking communion while knowing that I wasn't really a Christian would be provoking God beyond what was wise. Wasn't there biblical precedent for people being struck dead for less? So I went back to our long-suffering minister a couple of weeks beforehand and told him that I wouldn't be able to take first communion with the other children because I wasn't a Christian.

Exasperated, he said, "Kari, *of course* you're a Christian! Besides, if you don't take communion, you can't be confirmed." Which meant, of course, that I'd also miss out on my confirmation party and confirmation presents. That thought gave me pause.

After the next confirmation class, the minister asked me to stay behind. He told me he'd consulted with the members of the *Kirkerådet,* the church board, and they were willing for me to simply stay seated up at the front of the church while the other children took communion, and I could still be confirmed. "But think, Kari," he said. "All the congregation will be wondering why you're not taking communion with the others."

Maybe that's true, I thought, *but at least I won't be inviting Divine wrath in the form of lightning or other fatal event.*

So I was confirmed and I had my party and got my presents. But in my head, I heard a celestial clock ticking. The promise I'd made to God had been a solemn one—I had no thought of giving up my search for how to become a Christian—but I really had no idea where to turn to next.

Chapter 4

Steps to Christ

I T'S SURPRISING THE POWER THAT can be contained in something as simple as a schoolyard taunt. We humans are social creatures and often our strongest instinct when faced with conflict is to conform; to do whatever it takes to win the approval and acceptance of our peers. I've noticed that it doesn't matter if you're thirteen, thirty-three, or seventy-three years old, most of us have a "people-pleasing" reflex that can sometimes mess with our judgment and our decision-making.

It's a phenomenon that psychologists have long studied. In the 1950s, Solomon Asch, a Polish-American social psychologist, conducted a series of experiments that has since become famous. A young college student would be shown a number of lines on a piece of paper and then asked to identify the longest line. Immediately afterward, he would be taken into a room with a group of other participants (all of whom were "in" on the experiment—they were actors who had been primed ahead of time).

Each actor viewed the same series of lines and was asked to say out loud which line was longest. One by one, each of the actors gave an *incorrect* answer. Finally, the real participant was asked to identify the longest line. Over the course of the experiments, a full 75 percent of participants denied the reality of their own eyes at least once, and went along with the group answer, even though it was patently wrong!*

I think this impulse must have been alive and well in the days of

---

* Solomon E. Asch, "Opinions and Social Pressure," *Readings About the Social Animal* (1955), 17–26.

the early Christian church—I hear echoes of it in the words of the apostle Paul as he writes to the believers in the Roman province of Galatia. "Am I now trying to win the approval of human beings, or of God? Or am I trying to please people? If I were still trying to please people, I would not be a servant of Christ" (Galatians 1:10, NIV).

As I entered my fourteenth year, I was about to discover how difficult it could be to disregard the "approval of human beings" in my quest to become a "servant of Christ."

A forbidden visit

In the summer following my confirmation into the Lutheran faith I learned how to dance, and I loved it. I'd heard about a big outdoor dance party that was to be held one Saturday night at a place not far from where two of my aunts lived and I was determined to attend.

My mother had two sisters: one of them we saw quite regularly, but the other one was *persona non grata* within our family. She belonged to a strange religion called the Seventh-day Adventist Church, and my father didn't like us to have much to do with her.

My non-Adventist aunt, *tante* Anne, lived more than half an hour's walk away from my other aunt, *tante* Kalla. On the day of the dance, I traveled by train to my aunts' farming community, had a wonderful time at the party, and afterward slept that night at my *tante* Anne's house.

I woke the next day to a beautiful sunny Sunday morning and I suddenly thought that I might like to go and visit my "black-listed" aunt.

I'm so close to her house and I've hardly ever seen her, I thought. *Besides, I'm not going to let anyone tell me who I can or cannot visit, especially when it's my own aunt!*

Looking back, I'm convinced that the timing of my visit was God-led. I had no way of knowing that the Adventist church where my aunt worshiped was celebrating its tenth jubilee that weekend. In a country such as Norway, with its state-run and supported church, this group of Adventist believers in a remote farming community had not only established a congregation, but they'd also set up a church school—something that was almost unheard of.

I arrived at my *tante* Kalla's house to find a group of young people in the garden, sitting around singing hymns to the accompaniment of a young man playing the guitar.

How very embarrassing! I thought, and my immediate impulse was to retreat as quickly and as far as possible.

Sometimes, the future direction of one's life can turn on a single moment. One such moment came for me when someone in the group noticed me in the very act of turning to escape, and called me to come over and join them.

Well, now it was too embarrassing for me to leave! *Kari, you've surely got yourself in an awkward situation now,* I thought. I reluctantly joined the group and they went out of their way to make me feel welcome. Soon, I began to wonder if these Adventists weren't quite as strange as I'd been led to believe.

One man I met that afternoon was the church school teacher, Thoralf Fønnebø, and he asked me about where I went to school and my favorite subjects. That was easy—I was completely besotted with reading and so I talked with him about some of the books I liked.

"Kari, we're having another get-together this evening at our home and we'd love you to come too," he said. "Plus, I have a few books I'd like to lend you that I think you might enjoy." I wasn't too sure about meeting up with the group again, but I certainly wasn't going to lose the opportunity to get my hands on some new books, and so I said I'd come along.

I don't remember the titles of two of the books the church school teacher gave me that evening, but the words on the cover of the third book immediately grabbed my attention. *Steps to Christ.* For someone who had been searching for a path to Christianity, this was an intriguing title, to say the least.

It didn't take me long to devour the book. It was beautifully written, filled with ideas I'd never encountered before, and the tone was so warm and reassuring. Yet it left me feeling somewhat bewildered.

Really? I thought. *That's it? Can becoming a Christian be* that *simple?* I was dubious, so I read the book through again.

It can't possibly be that easy! I said to myself. *I have to get myself back there to my aunt's friends so I can ask them some questions about this.*

But it was some time before I could return to my aunt's house. In the first place, the train trip cost money, and in the second, I had to find some plausible excuse for going to visit my non-Adventist aunt. I couldn't just announce to my parents that I was going to visit *tante* Kalla.

In the meantime, I read the other books Mr. Fønnebø had lent me and I again encountered the concept of the Sabbath—but this time it all made sense to me. The author explained both the biblical basis for the Sabbath and the process by which the day had been changed to Sunday, and why the seventh day of the week should still be kept holy.

I did manage to visit my aunt again before too long, and I spent some time talking through my many questions with the church school teacher. He enrolled me in a Voice of Prophecy Bible correspondence course, and so every time throughout that school year that I was able to get to *tante* Kalla's house, I did my Bible correspondence study and talked with the school teacher.

I still remember the very first Sabbath I spent in that small Adventist congregation. The program began with something they called "Sabbath School," in which they discussed a topic they all seemed to have studied throughout the week. They frequently discussed different Bible verses, but every so often, they referred also to "Sister White."

I studied English at school, so I knew that "White" was an English surname. *How can it be that so many of these Adventists married someone named "White"?* I wondered. At the first opportunity, I put my question to the church school teacher, Mr. Fønnebø. I suspect he probably had a good laugh later, but he kindly set me straight on the "Sister White" issue with just a hint of a smile.

Leaving home

By Christmas, I'd come across the biblical concept of clean and unclean foods, and it seemed to me, as I then understood the Bible, that not eating pork was an expression of obedience to the Written Word.

Christmas at our home was a time when Mother made a special effort to make everything pleasant and inviting, and this year, 1949, was no exception. On Christmas Eve, we always had a delicious dish called *rømmegrøt,* or sour cream porridge, and for lunch Mother always cooked rutabaga, potatoes, and the centerpiece of the meal was a traditional Norwegian dish of salt-cured and boiled pigs' trotters.

"Mother, just give me some rutabaga and potatoes," I said as my mother began serving.

I'd been trying to speak quietly but my strange request caught Father's ears.

"Kari, if you don't like the food we have here you may leave the table," he said.

Unwisely, I said, "Well, I just don't think pork is good for me, that's all."

There was a long silence. Father wasn't stupid and he said, "What is all this about? Have you been out to see *tante* Kalla?"

"Yes," I said.

Another silence, this one darker and more ominous. "Well then, you can leave this house," said Father, and his tone brooked no argument or discussion.

There was a train leaving at 3:30 that afternoon and Mother helped me pack a small suitcase. She didn't want me to go but she didn't dare go against Father's command. She told me to go and stay at the house of my non-Adventist aunt, *tante* Anne, who had recently moved to the village of Hjuksebø, just one stop up the railway line from the train station near our home.

So on the night of Christmas Eve, I knocked on my aunt and uncle's door and asked them to take me in. Through their kindness, I was given a home and was able to continue attending my high school by catching the train back to Notodden each morning.

Against All Odds

I studied hard. The school week at all the state-run schools in Norway included Saturdays, so I couldn't attend my *tante* Kalla's church, but I got away as often as I could on Sundays to continue my Bible studies with the church school teacher.

Somehow the other kids at school discovered that I was studying with the Adventists, and the teasing began.

"Kari, did you know that Adventists wash each others' feet in juice?" they asked me.

Or, "Kari, are you planning to let the Adventists baptize you? You'd better be careful. When you want to become an Adventist, they go out and dig a hole in the frozen lake. They put you down there and when you're just about to drown, they let you up again."

My response to their teasing was less-than-Christian. If I hadn't known it before, I soon discovered that I had a fiery temper, and my tormenters discovered that I could give as good as I got.

This presented me with a new dilemma. I felt that I was getting so close to finally becoming a "real Christian," yet I had a suspicion that Christians had better control over their tempers than I did over mine.

The train I caught to school every morning arrived more than an hour before classes began. I was a good student and ahead in my studies, so I used the extra time to help some of my classmates who were lagging behind in math, English, and German.

These early morning tutoring sessions sometimes ended in teasing from some of the kids, and inevitably I'd lose my temper. One morning I decided that I needed a change of plan, so instead of heading for the classroom, I headed for the bathroom.

In the girls' bathroom there were seven stinky toilet stalls in a row, and I locked myself in one and there I sat from 7:30 to 8:30 until classes began. Both girls and boys came knocking at the door. "Please, Kari, won't you come out and help us with our school work?" they asked.

"No, I'm not coming out because I know I'll get angry," I said.

"We won't tease you anymore, we promise," they said.

"No, it's not your problem, it's mine," I replied. And so there I sat for I don't know how many mornings. I'm not sure if it was the atrocious smell, or simply the chance to sit and reflect, but after some time I felt able to rejoin the other kids in the mornings with my temper reasonably in check.

For almost two years, I'd been studying the Bible, learning to pray and feeling increasingly sure that I was finally on the right track toward fulfilling my vow to the Lord to become a Christian.

It bothered me that I hadn't been able to attend church every Sabbath—legally, anyone younger than sixteen years of age had to have their parents' permission before requesting an exemption from Saturday school attendance. But even once I'd turned sixteen, there were still challenges. Soon after my birthday, I visited the school principal to tell him I wouldn't be attending Saturday classes anymore.

He looked at me and shook his head. "Kari, you are an excellent student," he said. "And because of that I will do everything in my power to make sure you don't end up joining that American sect. If there is an exam scheduled on Saturday in one of your classes, I won't request an exemption for you." His warning was serious—if I didn't sit for one of my exams, I wouldn't able to graduate from high school.

In the months that followed, I prayed that there would never be an important exam scheduled on Sabbath, and there never was.

A foretaste of heaven

In the summer of 1951, my horizons were dramatically expanded by an unexpected event. I wasn't a baptized member of the Adventist Church, yet someone in the little congregation I visited—I've never been able to discover who—decided to pay my way to a Europe-wide Adventist youth congress to be held in Paris in July.

It was a thrilling, disorientating experience. After a long train journey from Oslo, I walked through the tall iron gates of the *Parc des Expositions* down a long avenue of maple trees toward the main exhibition hall, hearing around me scraps of excited conversation in English, German, French, Swedish, Spanish, and other languages I couldn't quite recognize. I had suddenly gone from knowing barely a handful of Adventist young people, to standing among a crowd of more than six thousand young people from twenty-five countries, lifting the roof of the vast exhibition hall with the strength of our singing. I can still hear the beautiful, resonant voice of Pastor Edwin Lennard Minchin, Northern European Division youth leader, as he led us in songs such as "He Lives" and "Jesus Is Coming Again."

For me, it was a completely new experience in spiritual solidarity and camaraderie. Here were young people like me, earnestly looking for a closer walk with their Lord. Of course, I also met a few who seemed preoccupied with less weighty concerns, like clothes or boys. But it was clear that the vast majority of these young people were serious about the motto of the congress: *"Leve-toi, Eclaire le monde,"* "Arise, Shine!" They genuinely wanted to let the love of Christ shine through their worship and their lives. It was a revelation to me.

Our accommodations, were less than five star—we slept on old canvas army stretchers laid out in long rows on a huge dirt-floored hall. Our washing facilities consisted of a long pipe with strategically placed holes along its length, through which dripped steady streams of water. The toilet facilities? Well, they didn't bear thinking of. Yet, it didn't matter. I had a vivid foretaste of the glory of heaven in the spiritual fellowship of those five days in Paris.

Not one, but three

Tante Anne's husband, Sveinung, was an engineer for the railroad and during the week he lived and worked in a distant town, coming home only on the weekends. Apparently, in the town where he stayed, he'd seen an advertisement for some Adventist meetings and without telling his wife, he began attending and then embarked on a course of Bible study. Although he said nothing about what he was doing during the week, there were some unexplained changes in his behavior that didn't escape my aunt's notice.

"Kari, will you come to the cinema with me?" my aunt asked one Saturday afternoon. "There's a good movie showing tonight that I want to see."

"No," I said, "you know I don't go to the cinema anymore."

"I just don't understand anyone in this house," she said. "You won't go with me—all you ever do is sit here reading that stupid Bible. And now Sveinung tells me that *he* won't go to the movies with me either. I'm fed up with you both."

Whenever I could get away and whenever I could afford the train fare, I traveled to *tante* Kalla to visit with the Adventist group. In the warmth of that small congregation, I'd found a spiritual and emotional home—a place of safety that I had longed for.

There finally came a day when I became convinced that God really *did* love me, and I was determined that I would become a baptized Seventh-day Adventist. The following Saturday, I headed for church.

We met in rented rooms—the kitchen and living room of a young widow. The congregation of about thirty was made up of laborers, small-time farmers, and homemakers. To the casual observer, these were not people of any particular note. The surroundings were certainly not luxurious. The services and programs were simple.

But when chance brought me to this small group of Seventh-day Adventists, they "adopted" me. They didn't ask too many questions. They didn't criticize or tell me what I was doing wrong. As I'd studied the Bible and allowed God, inch by inch, into my life, they'd given me a safe haven and for this, I was profoundly grateful.

As I entered the room, I was startled to see an unexpected face— my uncle had also decided to begin attending church that week. I think he was as surprised to see me as I was to see him. But God hadn't finished yet. When my *tante* Anne discovered her husband's interest in church, she became curious and three weeks later began joining us each Sabbath. My aunt, uncle, and I were all baptized together on the same day in August 1951.

I was now seventeen years old and I was amazed as I looked back at the turns my life had taken since the winter I'd lay, weak and afraid, in my hospital bed recovering from heart surgery.

But if I thought the Lord had reached the limit of His capacity to surprise me, then the next few years were to prove me wrong.

45

Chapter 5

Growing in Grace

A s I LOOK BACK, I see clearly that the upheavals of my childhood and teenage years had instilled in me a sense of independence and a habit of facing problems head-on. For me, these were lessons born of necessity. My emotional, spiritual, and perhaps even physical, survival had so often depended on my willingness to take responsibility for myself and to embark on a course of action without the support or approval of others. I was probably born with a good, healthy streak of independence in my nature, but my life circumstances had certainly served to strengthen and grow this tendency.

Yet, the more time I spent with my new Seventh-day Adventist church family, the more I realized that being a Christian—that goal for which I'd strived for so long—meant living in *community* with other people. And that meant being accountable to others, being willing to defer to each other for the sake of harmony and—to be honest—being willing to put up with each other's various quirks and inconsistencies. Rather than the fierce independence that had taken me thus far in life, I now found that a spirit of *inter*dependence was what was needed.

In the years since, I've come to understand that the ideal model for Christian community finds its genesis in the very nature of the Godhead; that divine relationship between the Father, Son, and Holy Spirit. For instance, think in Scripture where God says, "Let *us* make man in *our* image, after *our* likeness" (Genesis 1:26, KJV; emphasis added). There's a foundation of mutuality there; a repudiation of self-reliance; an acknowledgement of perfect interdependence. Of course, when this perfect pattern for community is transposed into the everyday, imperfect reality of the church, it's not always smooth sailing.

As a newly minted member of the Adventist Church, I soon learned two important lessons about Christian community that have stayed with me. One lesson was positive, the other lesson brought with it profound disappointment.

First, I learned the powerful role that spiritual and emotional mentors can play in one's life, helping you through the hard times and deepening your spiritual roots.

Second, I learned that my new church wasn't perfect; I'd imagined it to be a veritable Garden of Eden, but I'd forgotten that even *that* Garden had its resident serpent.

New horizons

It was 1951 and I was seventeen years old. I was still estranged from my father and I continued to live in the home of my aunt and uncle. I'd finished at Notodden High school, but I still had a deep hunger for more education.

I had a new faith and a new sense of purpose in my spiritual life, but my material situation left much to be desired. I had no money and I was becoming increasingly aware that I couldn't stay at my aunt and uncle's house forever.

What did the future hold for me? I had no idea.

During this time of uncertainty, two women in particular at the Adventist church where I worshiped became my strongholds. The first was Maj-Britt, a Swedish woman who sang beautifully and played the guitar. She was married to the church schoolteacher—the one who'd first signed me up for the Voice of Prophecy Bible lessons. Maj-Britt had a motherly touch and dispensed warmth and good advice in equal measures.

A second woman, Tulla, was also a spiritual inspiration to me. She had grown up with the stigma of illegitimacy—a terrible burden in those days. But she exuded a sense of such peace and joy. She would recite long portions of Scripture, sing hymns, and recall passages from the writings of Ellen White.

Against All Odds

Between these two "mothers in Israel," I gained a sense of calm and stability, and began to make plans for my future. The schoolteacher and his wife suggested I go to work at the church's Hultafors Sanatorium in Sweden, a day's journey away by train. I wrote to the sanatorium, and received word back, saying, "Come, we have work for you as a nurses' aide."

I embarked on my adventure on September 1, 1951. For an untraveled, rural girl, that day-long train trip to Sweden may just as well have been an expedition to China. Marco Polo had nothing on me.

I changed trains in Oslo and Gottenberg, and by the time I arrived at Hultafors at eight in the evening, the station was closed and my trip was beginning to feel less like an adventure than a nightmare. I stepped off the train and looked along the platform for the person from the sanatorium who I'd been assured would meet me. The station was deserted.

I walked up and down the platform a few times then checked out the front of the station in case my contact was waiting for me there. There was no one.

I spoke only Norwegian—and an obscure dialect of Norwegian at that—and I didn't even know where the sanatorium was located or how far away it was.

I caught sight of man a little way up the platform—a railway signalman—and I moved quickly to accost him before he could disappear. It soon became clear, however, that we may as well have come from different planets. He spoke only a local Swedish dialect and neither of us had any idea what the other was saying. In desperation, I kept repeating the name of my destination: "Hultafors Adventist Sanatorium." Finally, he gathered what I wanted and he pointed to a road leading up the side of a steep hill.

By 1951, Hultafors Sanatorium already had a long and storied history. The first buildings of the sanatorium were constructed in 1889 and in the years since it had expanded in size and services and had built up an excellent reputation as a spa and health resort. It especially catered to those with cardiovascular disease. It offered a strict vegetarian diet, hydrotherapy treatments, and a beautiful location among pine trees overlooking an alpine lake. It had become a nationally renowned facility for those trying to shed weight and regain health.

I walked up the zigzagged road, carrying my suitcase, and with every step I felt more lonely and lost.

Finally, through the trees I caught a glimpse of the sanatorium buildings and I was overwhelmed with relief. I'd made it! And, even better, the first person I met was a young girl who spoke Norwegian. She found out where my room was and helped me settle in. I was assigned to share a room with a girl who spoke only Finnish—we couldn't understand each other at all—but it didn't matter to me. I was just delighted to finally be among other young people who shared my faith.

The Norwegian girl invited me to a party the following evening to meet some of the other young people. "It'll be at a house way back in the woods," she said. "Just walk back as far as you can and you'll find it."

There had been no young people in the little church back in Norway, so this was like a whole new world opening up to me. Here were Adventist young people—we believed the same things, they wouldn't tease me about my "strange beliefs." I could relax and be myself and for the first since the Paris youth congress, just enjoy being with other teenagers.

We aren't angels

I looked forward to that party. I made my way along the path through the woods until I found the little house with its lights ablaze. As I knocked on the door, I heard music coming from inside; music that sounded strangely familiar. As the door opened, the sound burst out and I recognized it immediately as dance music. The glimpse I caught of the young people inside made it clear that this was, indeed, a dancing party, and my heart just fell.

My Norwegian friend came to the door and gestured to me to come inside. In confusion, I said, "But this isn't what I thought—I can't come in."

"Don't be so silly, Kari," she said. "We're just having fun—harmless fun. Come inside, you'll see."

I had no words, so I simply turned and retraced my steps through the woods.

It's difficult even now to describe what I felt. From the time I'd vowed to God to become a Christian, to the time I was finally baptized into the Seventh-day Adventist Church, I felt I'd been caught up in a never-ending struggle. I'd faced down my father and been exiled from my home; I'd endured the teasing of my school friends; I'd stubbornly continued to meet and study with that "strange group" of Adventists.

Over the years of my spiritual quest, I'd also given up certain things and it hadn't always been easy. The unclean meat had gone first. But over the following months and years, I'd also stopped going to the cinema—a difficult sacrifice at the time. I'd stopped wearing jewelry and adopted a plainer way of dressing and doing my hair. And yes, I'd given up my beloved dancing as well.

In that walk through the woods back to my room at Hultafors Sanatorium, I found myself caught in the grip of profound disillusionment.

What have I done? I asked myself. *Could it be that I've upended my life—given up so much, and endured so much—for a sham faith? How else could Adventist young people so brazenly do what I've been taught is wrong?*

I cried myself to sleep and in the morning woke up just as discouraged.

Over the next few days, as I learned my new duties at the sanatorium and got to know some of the other staff, my mind kept churning. I was just an infant in the faith, and I began to wonder if perhaps I'd be better to simply write off my whole experience with the Adventist Church as a failure.

At some point during this time, I remembered Maj-Britt's final words to me before I'd left home for Sweden. At the time, her comment had made little impact on me. "Remember, Kari, you will find very few people in the church with wings," she had said. "And never forget that neither you nor I are angels either."

Maj-Britt could never have known how prescient her words would be. Of all the pieces of wisdom God has sent my way through the years, this simple truth about human nature has perhaps been the most important in my life. It's a truth that has come to my rescue many times, helping me to regain a proper sense of perspective in the face of events that could otherwise have led me into bitterness, resentment, or disillusionment.

As I went about my work at the sanatorium, I began to reflect that perhaps the dance party said more about individual human fallibility than it did about the authenticity of the community of faith I'd joined.

We're not perfect—none of us, I kept reminding myself. *And Kari, you're not exactly sprouting wings either!*

My disappointment remained, but the cords of trust and faith that bound me to my Savior stayed strong.

The Lord in His goodness didn't leave me without support. I went to prayer meeting later that same week and met a woman who also became a "mother in Israel" to me—a sixty-year-old physiotherapist called Sister Elsa. Her friendship got me through the long winter at Hultafors.

A new direction

I had to learn Swedish very quickly during my time at the sanatorium. I continued working there through the spring of 1952, but I'd made up my mind, come what may, that I'd find a way to continue my education.

I'd heard about an Adventist junior college in Norway, and so I set my sights on attending there when the new school year began in the autumn. I was so ignorant of church structure—I'd never heard of church conferences or unions. I didn't have access to the Norwegian church paper, either, so I hadn't read that the West Nordic Union had sold its junior college in Norway and was sending Adventist students from Norway to the church college in Denmark.

I sent off my application to the Adventist junior college in Norway and got a letter back telling me the school had closed. What the letter failed to mention was the fact that Norwegian Adventist students were now going to Denmark for their junior college education.

What was I to do now? I applied to the Adventist junior college in Sweden and was accepted. My next challenge was money—I had hardly any. I kept writing to my father to get his permission for me to go door-to-door over the summer selling Adventist books, but he kept refusing.

"Please, Father," I wrote to him again late that spring. "The only way I can get money to go to school is by canvassing. Won't you please let me go?"

I'll never know what changed his mind, but his response this time was different. "Well, OK," he wrote. "You've done everything else, so you might as well become a beggar, too." His ungracious words filled me with pure joy—I would get my longed-for chance to go to college.

I spent the summer canvassing in Sweden with a lovely Swedish girl named Marta and we made a formidable selling team, racking up the most sales of any our fellow canvassers. Soon I had enough money saved to begin school.

A few weeks before I was due to leave, however, I got word that my application to the Norwegian junior college had somehow been transferred to the Danish Adventist junior college. Now I was being offered a place at the junior college in Denmark.

Should I go to Sweden as planned, or to Denmark, where I'd be with some of my fellow Norwegians?

The start date for the school in Denmark was earlier, and I still had to deliver some of the books I'd sold over the summer. So I wrote to the school registrar in Denmark saying I'd come if I could be two weeks late. He agreed, so my course was set.

I sometimes wonder how my life would have gone if I'd chosen to stick with my original plan and gone to the junior college in Sweden. What friends would I have made? What course of study would I have eventually pursued? Where would I have ended up living and working? Who would I have married? Would I have married at all?

Marriage, to my seventeen-year-old mind, was a risky business indeed. I'd seen, close up, what can happen when a marriage turns sour and I had no desire to experience that again in any form. The memories were too fresh: the harsh words, the raised voices, the physical abuse, the emotional damage to children who got caught in the cross fire of marital war.

I had long ago decided that marriage definitely wasn't for me.

In the late summer of 1952, as I packed up my few clothes and books and headed to Denmark to begin junior college, I was about to meet someone who would eventually change my mind.

Chapter 6

Baptism of Fire

I'VE ALWAYS HAD A STRONG "radar sense" for the misfits and nonconformists in any gathering—probably because, as the old saying goes, "It takes one to know one." I know from experience that it can be mystifying to stand at the edge of a group, faintly aware of unwritten codes of behavior, assumed knowledge, and a shared, unspoken history; and to wonder, *What exactly will it take for me to fully belong?*

I doubt there's a person alive who hasn't, at one time or another, experienced that unsettling feeling of "otherness."

"I'm not wearing the right clothes"; "I don't speak the same 'language'—I'm not on the right wavelength to talk easily with these people"; "I don't fit the right 'profile' (in terms of education, or social or financial status) to be a part of this group."

And so we allow ourselves to retreat to the margins and to take up a position of spectator rather than participant in the group. Or, if our sense of alienation becomes unbearable, we walk away.

I like to think that Jesus' ministry on earth carries a strong theme of "misfit theology." I love His discussion in Luke 14:7–14 of "dinner party etiquette." He says that those who put themselves forward and commandeer seats at the head of the table may find themselves unexpectedly humbled. And those who are hanging back diffidently on the edges of the group may find themselves led to the seats of honor at the head of the table. In the *Message* version of this passage, Jesus admonishes His listeners to think beyond their comfortable cliques. He says when you put on a dinner, "don't just invite your friends and family and rich neighbors, the kind of people who

54

will return the favor. Invite some people who never get invited out, the misfits from the wrong side of the tracks."

Unfortunately, life inside the church doesn't always resemble the divine template for community that Jesus gave us. We don't always look out for those who are a little uncertain—who are hanging back because they're not sure exactly what's needed to become part of the "club." It is so very easy to content ourselves with our own circle of friends and to enjoy comfortable fellowship with them.

But when we're willing to put ourselves out for someone else, to draw them into community with God's people, I believe this is a spiritual act of the highest order—it's a sacred gift that can make the difference between whether someone stays or goes.

I feel passionately about this because as a new Adventist, I so often identified strongly with Jesus' misfits—someone from "the other side of the tracks." Baptism into God's family had been a first, essential step in my spiritual journey. But, in many ways, just as significant was my "baptism of fire" into Adventism's unspoken traditions and assumed codes of behavior—all those subtle things that marked one as either an insider or an outsider.

A dream realized

On my train journey to Denmark, I was torn between anticipation and sheer terror. On the one hand, I was headed for a new country with an unfamiliar language where I knew not one soul. Yet, on the other hand, I would finally have the opportunity to study at an Adventist school—and to study theology at that!

The train carried me from Malmö, Sweden, toward the Danish capital of Copenhagen, and from there I took a train west and caught a ferry service across the strait known as the "Great Belt," a span of water that divides Denmark in half. On the other side, I caught a train northward to the picturesque village of Daugård.

The Danish Adventist Junior College at Daugård—called Vejlefjordskolen—is a small, beautiful campus set among rolling forested hills, not far from the calm waters of Vejle Fjord. When I arrived, school had already been in session for two weeks, and I realized immediately I had some catching up to do.

One of the first classes I attended was in Old Testament prophets, taught by biblical scholar V. Norskov Olsen. So many students had enrolled in this class that it couldn't be held in one of the regular classrooms and we met instead in the ladies lounge. I settled into one of the deep, cushioned armchairs and looked around the room, noting in passing the tall, blond young man who occupied the armchair to my right.

Professor Olsen began his lecture and it quickly became apparent that, for me, he may just as well have delivered it in Swahili. There are many similarities between the Norwegian and Danish languages and it's relatively easy to pick up the gist of what's being said. But there are significant differences when it comes to denoting numbers above fifty. Professor Olsen had chosen this day to focus on the reigns of various kings recorded in the Old Testament and the mass of dates he referenced made his lecture almost unintelligible to me.

I've never been blessed with the ability to hide my emotions behind a poker face and I suspect my utter befuddlement was written clearly across every feature. *What have I gotten myself into?* I thought. *I don't belong here!*

And then I sensed a movement on my right and I heard someone whispering, "Don't worry about it—I'll explain all the numbers to you later."

I soon got to know this young man—Jan Paulsen—and we struck up a friendship that grew out of a mutual love of talking. We talked about anything and everything—politics, current events, religion. We disagreed probably more often than we agreed, but no matter what we discussed, we challenged and stretched each other's thinking.

Jan soon brought me up to speed on Danish numbers—a topic that the Norwegian students had dealt with in the weeks before I'd arrived on campus. But in spite of this, I found a significant strike against me in the academic stakes. I had been determined to study theology—this is what I had longed for and worked toward—but my background in basic religious concepts and Scripture was very limited. I hadn't been steeped in these things from birth, through family worships and weekly Sabbath School attendance. Adventism wasn't part of my "DNA," as it seemed to be for so many of the students at Vejlefjordskolen. I had a constant sense that I was somehow on the outside looking in. But I studied hard—forgoing some of the social activities—and kept my grades high.

For some time after my arrival at the school, I felt somewhat like an anthropologist observing the customs and traditions of some remote tribe. I was a spectator—just looking on rather than really feeling like a legitimate member of the group. There was just too much in my past experience, I thought, that separated me from these seemingly untroubled young men and women, and I could not feel truly at home.

As the months passed, though, I began to lose my sense of being a "foreigner." The wonderful daily worship services and Sabbath programs, which I drank in eagerly, played a large part in this process. The singing and music were wonderful. When I sat with the other students in chapel, our voices blended together in a beautiful Danish hymn, I felt a peace that's hard to describe.

I lived up on the third floor of the women's dormitory, and also living on that floor was a teacher at the school named Esther Paulson. I suspect she sensed in me someone who could use a friend and mentor. I had plenty of determination and a good measure of audacity, but I wasn't very old and I didn't have much experience. My growing friendship with Esther provided me with a spiritually mature, generous counselor. Her infectious laugh and her ready words of encouragement and advice were exactly what I needed—especially when, in my second year, I was asked to be an assistant dean. With Esther's help, my spiritual roots grew stronger and deeper.

"He isn't for you"

My canvassing the summer before had earned me enough money to cover tuition, but I still needed to work for pocket money, enough to cover things such as toothpaste and other essentials. For the first year of school, I worked in the laundry and did cleaning work for the wife of the school principal, Mrs. Varmer. Every Friday I polished the wood floors of her home until they shined with a high gleam, and then I'd place newspapers down to protect my work from muddy shoes. I can still hear the sharp voice of Mrs. Varmer when her husband would wander blithely onto the freshly cleaned surface. "Aksel, Aksel don't you *dare* step on that floor!"

Every Friday she made a special applesauce and cream dessert for Sabbath and after I'd finished my cleaning, she would sit me down at the kitchen table and serve me a small dish of this delicious pudding. She was a former school teacher, kind, but with a very stern manner, and so it was with some trepidation that I heard her say one day, "Kari, sit down at the table—I have something to talk to you about."

"What's that?" I asked.

"It's come to my knowledge that you're becoming friendly with Jan Paulsen," she said. "I don't think that's a very good idea. I've noticed that he doesn't have enough to say for himself, and I feel that you're not suited—he's not the one for you."

During his childhood, Jan had struggled with a pronounced stutter. He still tended to be slower in delivering some of his comments and he rarely spoke up in class. Mrs. Varmer may have thought him too quiet, but with every conversation we had, it became evermore clear to me that Jan possessed an unusual depth of intelligence and perception.

Mrs. Varmer wasn't the only one to notice that Jan and I were spending more time together. We weren't boyfriend and girlfriend—I wasn't even remotely interested in that sort of relationship, I thought. We just liked to talk!

One day a girl said to me, "Kari, it's strange. You're such a 'goody goody,' but you go out walking with Jan Paulsen."

"What's wrong with walking with Jan Paulsen?" I asked, surprised.

"It's against the rules—didn't you know that?" she said.

Well, no, I didn't. I hadn't been schooled in the nuances of interactions between teenagers within Adventist circles.

Baptism of Fire

But sure enough, the principal of the college soon decided that our walking and talking violated the college rule that stated, "Students should not associate with the opposite sex in an obvious manner." From that time on, we were accompanied on our walks with a chaperone whose presence failed to dampen our enthusiasm for long, energetic discussions on every topic under the sun.

As the months went by and as more and more people began to notice the growing friendship between Jan and me, I began to sense a change in myself as well. A new element entered our relationship. We still talked and debated as fiercely as ever, but there was a growing realization that neither of us wanted the conversation between us to ever end.

One Sabbath afternoon, we joined a group of students for a long walk into the hills, and as we climbed a particularly steep part of the path, Jan took my hand to help me up and he didn't let go.

A new journey begins

We got engaged on May 11, 1954, the day of our graduation from junior college. As I look back from the perspective of a lifetime of shared experiences with Jan—times of joy, of heartbreak, and everything else in between—I see a very young, somewhat naïve couple, filled with love for each other, and anxious to get started on the adventure before them. We had no clear idea of the course we should chart, but we were supremely confident that the future would work out just fine because we'd face it together.

Before the graduation ceremony began, Jan and I both quietly left the crowded gymnasium and walked into a nearby beech forest. It was a beautiful, clear spring day and the sunlight filtered through the yellow green of the beech leaves as we pledged ourselves to each other and exchanged plain gold bands. These were our wedding rings, which in Scandinavia are traditionally worn on the left hand during the couple's engagement and swapped to the right hand during the marriage ceremony.

Perhaps it was the romance of the moment that inspired us, but on impulse we decided to dig a hole at the base of the tree where we'd become engaged, and bury the containers that had held our rings. We vowed that one day we'd return to that spot and dig up the containers. There was no need for us to mark the spot, we thought, for we'd never forget any detail of this moment.

Eleven years later, we did return to Vejlefjordskolen for a visit and at the first opportunity we walked into the forest, intent on retrieving these long-buried mementos of our engagement day. As we wandered through the forest, we quickly discovered, first, that one beech tree looks very much like any other beech tree, and second, that our memories of our engagement hadn't remained quite as crystal clear as we'd anticipated. And then it also struck us that even if we should be lucky enough to find the place we'd buried the ring boxes, they would have long since decomposed into nothingness! We laughed long and hard that day.

With graduation behind us, Jan and I made plans for the future and the event that dominated our horizon was Christ's soon return. We were both convinced that we needed to get moving; we needed to start working for the Lord quickly because time on earth was fast running out. Our wedding date was set for the following summer, so in the meantime, Jan accepted a call to work as a ministerial intern in Stavanger, southwestern Norway, and I traveled way up into the northeast of the country to work as a church school teacher and Bible instructor in the coastal town of Namsos.

Our separation wasn't easy and it was a relief to meet up again at Christmas, and then the following year at Easter time. By now, however, another challenge confronted us. All able-bodied young men in Norway were required to perform national military service, which meant training with firearms. As a conscientious objector, Jan would have the option instead to serve his time in a remote region of the country cutting timber or building roads—but the catch was that he'd have to serve eighteen months rather than the usual twelve. It wasn't an attractive idea for either of us.

Jan had recently gone for his compulsory military physical exam, and he'd "fortunately" been suffering at the time with a bad case of laryngitis, which pushed him down the list a little. But we knew he couldn't put off service indefinitely. There was one potential way to escape, however: if Jan was enrolled in a course of study, his service requirement would be automatically postponed for at least the duration of his course. So we decided that Jan needed to do further study.

There were two main options before us. Division church leaders were encouraging theology students from Norway to travel to Newbold College in England for further theological training and they offered some financial assistance. But from our perspective, this option was marred by the fact that the Newbold course of study was limited to a bachelor's degree.

On the other hand, if we could somehow find a way to travel to the United States, Jan could finish his bachelor's at the church's Emmanuel Missionary College in Berrien Springs, Michigan, and then go on to study at the seminary in Washington, D.C. This option came, however, with a significant drawback: the division would not offer any subsidy and Jan and I had barely one Norwegian krone to our names. With Jan working as a pastoral intern and me as a church school teacher, it was a significant stretch just to meet our individual weekly expenses, let alone put anything aside for after our marriage.

Yet with the optimism of youth faced with ridiculous odds, we decided that, come what may, Jan would study in the United States, and we set about making it happen.

Chapter 7

The New World

I N 1726, CLERGYMAN AND WRITER Jonathan Swift published his now classic work, *Gulliver's Travels,* a brash satire of the politics, religion, and popular thought of his time. Many of Swift's allusions to contemporary issues go over the heads of current-day readers (including me!), but most of us can still relate to the central character, Gulliver, as he bumbles his way through encounters with a variety of weird and wonderful cultures. There are the "Laputans," a race of people who are masters of scientific theory but have no ability to apply it in practical ways. There are the "Houyhnhnms," strange, arrogant horselike creatures who eventually reject Gulliver for being of a lower social order. Or there's the race of tiny people known as "Lilliputians," who are engaged in a fierce civil war over which end of a boiled egg one should open first—the larger end, or the smaller end.

To my mind, Gulliver's adventures are a spot-on expression of the phenomenon of culture shock—that disorientating feeling that occurs when our worldview begins to expand, and we start to realize that many of our cultural structures, which may have seemed so self-evident and stable, are constructed instead on a flimsy foundation of inconsistent, irrational, and quirky human nature.

When Jan and I decided to leave Scandinavia for the United States, we were both just twenty years of age. It was the 1950s—well before today's technology-fueled "global culture" that has managed to smooth away some of the more jagged edges of culture shock for today's younger generations.

The New World

In the years that have passed since our decision to leave Norway, Jan and I have made our home in a wide range of countries and cultures. We've lived among the Ashanti people of West Africa, whose rich traditions include one particularly intriguing feature—keeping Saturday, the seventh day, as a holy day of rest. We've lived among warring tribes in Nigeria and among the mannered academe of a German university town. We've spent many years, also, in Britain and the United States.

Then, during the eleven years that Jan was president of the Seventh-day Adventist world church, we traveled together to many different countries and experienced firsthand that amazing patchwork of ethnicities and cultures that gives such energy and life to our global family of faith.

But in 1955, we were innocents—perhaps those who are less kind may say "naïve."

Looking back, I realize that God was beginning His work of expanding our horizons and teaching us some lessons about culture and human nature that, later, would become so important.

A new family

So much had changed in my life since the Christmas Eve five years earlier when my father issued his ultimatum: either give up meeting with "those Adventists" or leave home. Yet, in the months before my wedding, I found myself once again writing to my father for permission to do something I knew he didn't want me to do.

Jan and I planned to be married on July 1, 1955—just three weeks short of my twenty-first birthday, when I'd be legally free to marry whom I pleased. But until then, I needed parental permission.

And so I wrote, "Father, will you please write a letter saying I can go ahead with my marriage to Jan?" According to my father's thinking, there were two black marks against Jan. First, he was from northern Norway—practically a foreigner. And, second, was the far more serious issue of Jan's religion and chosen profession. A Seventh-day Adventist pastor as a son-in-law? For my father, there could hardly have been anything more distasteful.

I don't know what persuaded my father to grant us his permission. Perhaps he was simply convinced I was beyond redemption, but he gave his reluctant blessing for the wedding to go ahead as scheduled. My mother and siblings, on the other hand, welcomed Jan wholeheartedly, in spite of my father's barely concealed hostility.

There was no reserve, however, in the acceptance Jan's family extended to me—they couldn't have been kinder or more gracious. I loved spending time in their home, which was filled with laughter and happy conversation. Jan's childhood experiences in this loving, warm Adventist family were a far cry from the constant tension that marked relationships in my family.

We were married in Jan's childhood hometown of Narvik, in the far north of Norway inside the Arctic Circle. In those days, churches couldn't legally marry couples, so we went first to the town hall for a civil ceremony, and then to the local Adventist church for a simple service of blessing. My sisters, nine and eighteen years old, were the only members of my family who attended.

A busman's honeymoon
Our honeymoon could be best described as "unorthodox." The Norwegian-America Line steamship the SS *Stavangerfjord* would depart Oslo for New York City on August 5, just five weeks after our wedding, and Jan and I were determined that he would be on board for the first leg of his journey to Emmanuel Missionary College in Berrien Springs, Michigan.

Our plan was to spend our honeymoon canvassing—selling Adventist books door-to-door—in an effort to raise enough money to pay for Jan's fare to America. Fortunately, we didn't have to worry about tuition costs—Jan had visited the Norwegian State Student's Loan Association and they'd agreed to grant him a loan for one year of his bachelor's degree in America. It was the first time this state agency had given assistance to a Seventh-day Adventist student training for the ministry.

The day after our wedding we caught the train south through Sweden to the Adventist publishing house in Oslo, where we borrowed two creaky old bicycles and were assigned a canvassing territory.

That summer of 1955 saw temperatures rise to almost tropical (for Norway) highs—it was hot! We rented a small room and each day we'd cycle to a bridge that spanned a swift-flowing river that followed the valley floor. On the bridge each morning we'd part ways—I'd go up the valley so I'd have the easier downhill route on the way back, while Jan would head down the valley to begin his canvassing route. We were so conscientious, focused on the volume of sales we knew we needed to pay for Jan's fare to New York City.

Those scrappy old bikes we'd borrowed meant that Jan and I dreaded every upward incline, but Norway is nothing but hills and mountains. Even without our door-to-door selling, it was dreadfully hot, tiring work just to get around.

One especially hot morning, about three weeks into our honeymoon, I began to have reoccurring visions of the clear, cool water of the river where Jan and I parted each morning. As I pedaled hard up hills and sweat ran in irritating rivulets down my back, that image of the river became even sharper in my mind.

"That's it! I'm taking a break," I said. I turned my bicycle around and headed back down the valley toward our rented rooms. I guiltily retrieved my swimsuit and headed toward the bridge. As I pedaled up over the last rise, I saw another bicycle leaning against the bridge railings. And as I got closer still, I saw a familiar figure luxuriating in the cool water, and I suddenly didn't feel so guilty for abandoning my work!

That afternoon, Jan and I enjoyed our spontaneous half-day holiday to the full, but the next morning we got back on our old bicycles and resumed our single-minded canvassing.

At the end of five weeks, we'd managed between us to raise enough money for Jan's boat fare to New York City, along with a Greyhound bus fare to Southbend, Indiana, and thirty dollars in cash for Jan's incidental expenses along the way.

I traveled with Jan to Oslo to see him board the SS *Stavangerfjord*. We'd been married for just five weeks and now we were saying goodbye for who-knew-how-long. At the end of the summer, after I'd finished delivering the books Jan and I had sold, I planned to return to Namsos to teach again at the church school and then work as a Bible instructor. We knew that on my small wage, it would be many months before we'd saved enough for me to join Jan in the United States.

Jan departed on his transatlantic journey, and I took a bus back to our canvassing territory and our rented room. I had less than thirty kroners—enough to buy a bit of food until I could get some more money by making book deliveries.

An unpromising start

I didn't know it until much later, but Jan's introduction to America was less than auspicious. During his nine-day voyage, Jan had become friendly with a fellow traveler—a Norwegian chemical engineer— who was planning to travel from New York City by Greyhound bus to the west coast of the United States. He was about thirty years old, older than Jan by about a decade.

Together they disembarked in New York City and caught a taxi to the Greyhound station to put their suitcases into storage so they could explore the city for a few hours until their buses departed. As they stood in line, chatting together, a man approached them, speaking Norwegian with an accent that marked his origins from southern Norway.

Jan and his friend were delighted to meet such a warm, friendly fellow-Norwegian, and were pleased when he offered to be their guide for the afternoon. "But I do have a quick errand to do first," he said. "My daughter is getting married and I need to pick up some silverware I've had engraved for her," said the man. "It won't take long, though."

As they continued talking, the man said, "Well, I don't have the cash with me to pick up the silverware, but if you're able to lend it to me, I'll quickly do that first so we can get on with our sightseeing. I'll withdraw the money from my bank to pay you back this afternoon."

He turned first to Jan's friend and asked if he had thirty dollars to lend him. "No," said the chemical engineer emphatically. "I do not!"

The man then turned to Jan, "Well, do *you* have the money to lend me? I'll pay you back almost straight away."

Jan, just twenty years old and an utterly unseasoned traveler, was caught in a quandary. He didn't want to lend his money, he was starting to feel very uneasy, but he simply couldn't lie. "Yes, I do have a bit less than thirty dollars—but that's all I have and it has to see me through until I get to Michigan," he said.

With profuse thanks, the man took the money and said, "I'll be back before you know it."

"Wait!" said the chemical engineer. "We're coming with you."

"No," he replied. "Stay here—I won't be long."

After an extended back-and-forth, it was decided that Jan would accompany him on his errand to pick up the silverware. As Jan glanced back, he noticed that his friend from the ship was following them at a discreet distance.

The man led Jan to a large building and when they came into the lobby, he said, "Wait here—I'll be back in just a moment with my silverware." But before he could move off, the chemical engineer came running through the door. "Stop!" he said. "Give Jan back his money."

It wasn't easy to persuade the man to give up his charade, but when the chemical engineer threatened to yell for the police, the man reluctantly pulled out his billfold. And as he extracted Jan's money, Jan could clearly see that the billfold was chock-full of cash! He told me later that he has rarely been so angry.

Jan's first letter to me from America contained the enigmatic comment, "Kari, something happened in New York—but I'll tell you about it in a later letter."

However, later never came. As Jan thought about it more, he realized that such a tale may discourage me from ever boarding a boat to America, and so for the next nine months I was destined to wonder about this mysterious "something" that had happened.

Together again

By March 1956, we had saved enough for me to purchase my

fare to join Jan at Emmanuel Missionary College in Berrien Springs, Michigan. Jan arranged for the Norwegian Adventist pastor in New York City to meet me at the docks and take me to the Greyhound station. The arrangement was that I would hold an umbrella in one hand and an Adventist publication, the *Norwegian Youth Instructor,* in the other—that was how the pastor would recognize me.

But while I was still traveling across the Atlantic, the Norwegian pastor contacted Jan and said, "I have to attend some conference meetings, but don't worry. I've arranged for the Swedish Adventist pastor to meet Kari."

After the first few days at sea, my voyage had degenerated into a haze of seasickness. I disembarked in New York City with profound gratitude and I stood, clutching my umbrella and magazine, waiting for the Norwegian pastor. My stomach was still churning.

A man came up, speaking in Swedish, and asked me if I'd had a nice trip. My reply to him was short and cold. *Why is this person bothering me?* I thought. To my consternation, though, he seemed disinclined to leave me alone and he continued to pepper me with cheerful questions and seemed unaffected by my increasingly rude responses.

"OK, then," he said to me finally. "We'd better get going."

"What!" I said in disbelief. "I'm not going anywhere with you!"

It didn't take long to sort out my misunderstanding but I was terribly embarrassed. When he suggested that we stop at a café for something to eat on the way to the Greyhound station, I felt I couldn't politely decline—even though food was the last thing my seasick stomach needed.

I sat across the table from the pastor, trying to keep up my end of the conversation, as the smell of food and the warmth of the restaurant began to oppress me. Our food arrived. I took a few bites, and then without any warning, was promptly sick all over the table.

It seemed that in America I'd developed an uncanny knack for embarrassing myself, and this tendency continued on the long bus trip to South Bend, Indiana, where Jan would meet me.

An older American couple in the seats across the aisle took pity on me. I was twenty-one years old, but I looked far younger and I suspect the turmoil I felt inside showed clearly on my face.

They asked me questions and listened kindly as I answered them slowly in my halting English. I may have been able to read Shakespeare and Dickens, but my conversational English was less-than-stellar and the nuances of many words escaped me.

"So, why are you traveling to Berrien Springs?" they asked.

"I'm going to meet my husband, who's a student at a college there," I replied.

"How lovely," they said. "And what is he studying?"

"He is studying to become a priest!" I said proudly.

There was a silence. Then, the husband leaned over toward me and said gently, "But Kari, priests don't have wives."

I was incensed. "Well, this one certainly does!" I declared.

The Norwegian word for *prest* covered the full range of clergymen, both Catholic and Protestant, and obviously didn't translate well into English. My error was soon sorted out and we were able to laugh about it together. But for me, the incident was yet another reminder that I'd entered "alien" territory. All my assumptions, all the social constants that had undergirded my life thus far, I could no longer simply take for granted.

I have no words to describe my happiness as I finally walked down the bus steps and saw Jan's face. Before long, my sense of optimism revived and I was ready for the adventure to continue. More particularly, I was anxious to finally see the campus of Emmanuel Missionary College—a place that had loomed large in my imagination for so long.

Chapter 8

A New Normal

BARBARA KINGSOLVER'S WELL-KNOWN NOVEL, *THE Poisonwood Bible*, paints a vivid and disturbing picture of what can happen when cultures collide. She writes of a fictional Baptist missionary from the United States who travels to the Belgian Congo in the late 1950s with his wife and their four daughters. The missionary has good intentions but is tone deaf when it comes to differences of language, values, and culture. His ongoing struggles to communicate are closely observed by one of his daughters, who sums up the problem this way: "Everything you're sure is right can be wrong in another place."*

In a pivotal scene that serves as a metaphor for the entire novel, the missionary attempts to preach in the local language. "Tata Jesus is bangala!" he declares, intending to say, "Jesus is 'precious.' " Yet, he is unaware that in the Kikongo language, intonation can radically change a word's meaning. And thus what he is really saying to his congregation is, "Jesus is poisonwood tree!"**

"Everything you're sure is right . . ."

When I left Norway for the United States, there were a lot of things I was sure were right. Some related, for instance, to customs and ways of doing things that I'd absorbed since childhood. Other "self-evident" values I carried with me across the Atlantic related to my Adventist faith. The small group of believers that had nurtured

---

* Barbara Kingsolver, *The Poisonwood Bible* (New York: Harper Collins 2002), 505.
** Ibid., 276.

my spiritual growth had also bequeathed to me certain ways of expressing my faith. At the time, I simply accepted these things as universal principles—the "way things were." In Scandinavia, for example, church members usually greeted each other with the prefix of "Sister" or "Brother" and this courtesy, I assumed, was the usual mode of address throughout the world church.

Christmas trees? These were utterly pagan and to display one in one's home would be a shocking thing. Makeup? Elaborate hairstyles? These were strictly out of keeping with the modesty required of an Adventist woman. (In fact, the good members of my home congregation had probably done too good a job of teaching me to reject "adornment." I remember in my teens coming upon the site of a terrible train accident near my home where some of the carriages had left the track. I glimpsed among the wreckage the awful sight of a woman lying in the snow, obviously dead. And she was wearing nail polish . . . It was a double horror to me.)

It's easy to look back and wince at the narrow worldview of my younger self. But my desire to know God's will and to do it was entirely in earnest.

To me, "American Adventism" was a new and sometimes startling phenomenon, and with its embrace of Christmas, national flags raised in church sanctuaries, women who had different ideas about modesty in dress. I soon realized that although Seventh-day Adventists share a common language of faith, we all tend to speak it with our own national and cultural "intonations" or "accents."

So when it comes to the language of faith, how does one safely sift eternal values from cultural padding?

I have no easy answer to give, but my journey within Adventism has left me with one deeply held belief—that any attempt to judge the motives or spirituality of another human being is a dead-end proposition.

Spiritual arrogance about dress, diet, entertainment, or whatever inflicts terrible damage within the body of Christ. I love the way Dietrich Bonhoeffer says it in *The Cost of Discipleship:* "By judging others, we blind ourselves to our own evil and to the grace which others are just as entitled to as we are."* (This principle comes in especially handy when dealing with teenagers who need to be reminded of God's grace probably more than they need reminders about standards of behavior.)

When I look to the Christ of Scripture, I can't help but conclude that *people matter more than anything.* Any intervention on our part in someone else's spiritual walk must be motivated and disciplined by a redemptive spirit—and this isn't as easy as it may sound. Christ's example tells me no matter what higher spiritual or moral ground I occupy (or think I occupy), my very first duty is to demonstrate God's loving care for frail and hurting people.

It's not always easy—and it's certainly not our normal, human inclination. I think of Jesus' encounter with the social outcast Zacchaeus, who was not someone any "righteous" person would choose to associate with. He was beyond the pale—grasping, greedy, and profiting from the Roman subjugation of the Jewish people in Palestine. Yet, in the biblical account, you just can't help but sense the gentle kindness—even respect—that Jesus extends to this pariah. "When Jesus reached the spot, he looked up and said to him, 'Zacchaeus, come down immediately. I must stay at your house today.' . . . All the people saw this and began to mutter, 'He has gone to be the guest of a "sinner" ' " (Luke 19:5–7, NIV).

Jesus wasn't patronizing. And He didn't reel off an indictment of Zacchaeus's many moral failings. Instead, He spoke to this fallen human being directly, kindly, and with compassion, showing us clearly that every person—even the least righteous among us—is innately valuable and worthy of respect. Jesus showed us time and time again that our value accrues not because of what we do or achieve, but simply because we are God's creation. Every human being thus has God-given dignity and value and the potential to live with Him eternally. When we allow this truth to enter our hearts, how can we dare to feel superior to any other person?

---

* Dietrich Bonhoeffer, *The Cost of Discipleship* (New York: Touchstone, 1995), 185.

A New Normal

Closer to heaven

The mid-1950s was an exhilarating time to be on the campus of Emmanuel Missionary College. In 1955, when Jan arrived, there were some thirteen hundred students enrolled—eight hundred on the Berrien Springs campus—representing thirty-two U. S. states and eighteen foreign countries. Under the leadership of Dr. Floyd O. Rittenhouse, EMC was in the throes of expansion: within the space of a few years a new music building was erected, extra accommodation added for women students in Lamson Hall, and there was the grand opening of both a new Life Science Building and a new Agricultural center. Every weekend saw concerts and events, as well as student evangelistic efforts in nearby towns. There was an ongoing fund-raising drive, also, for the first-ever campus church building for students.

In short, EMC was a beehive of multiculturalism and youthful energy that seemed to have been incongruously plunked down in the midst of a sleepy, staid midwestern farming community. For two immigrants from Norway, who up until that point had had limited contact with the larger Adventist community, this was close to heaven.

A new home

One of the first people Jan met when he got off the bus at Berrien Springs was a Norwegian lady he knew—the wife of one of the students. He told her he was on his way to register as a student.

"Don't ask for accommodation in one of the dorms," she advised, "because you won't be able to get out as much to work and earn money. Come home with us until you can find a place of your own!"

So Jan registered as a married student with the college, but he stayed with his Norwegian friends and began hunting for an apartment. He met up with another Norwegian student—a teacher who'd once taught at the school where I'd become an Adventist. Together, they decided to find a place to rent and share costs until I arrived.

They found a small apartment and furnished it simply. Jan bought a secondhand sofa bed and his friend bought a mattress and box spring. But within days of moving into their new home, both of them began to itch.

Jan suspected he knew the cause. Growing up in North Norway during the war, he'd never seen or tasted fruit such as apples, oranges, or bananas. When he'd traveled to Paris in 1951 to attend the division-wide youth congress, his eye had been caught by the sight of fruit piled high in the windows of *magasins de fruits*. He'd bought himself a big bag of grapes, which he promptly devoured. Almost immediately, he had an allergic reaction and broke out in hives.

So Jan said to his friend, "It's from fruit—we're eating too much fruit." Yet although they cut back on their fruit eating, the itchiness continued.

One night Jan woke up to see his friend with the light on, frantically beating at his mattress, and the cause of their itching soon became clear. So began a prolonged battle to rid their bedding of the insects they'd inherited. They ended up throwing out the mattress, but tried to save the sofa bed by spraying it repeatedly with insecticide. Unfortunately, while the fumigation drove away the bugs, it left behind a strong odor. When I finally joined Jan in Berrien Springs and he led me through the door of our new home, my first words were, "Jan, it smells *really* different in here." To my great annoyance, Jan and his friend laughed long and hard, but it wasn't until much later that I finally learned the awful truth about that smell.

Back to the hospital

By saving and planning, we'd managed to get ourselves from Norway to Emmanuel Missionary College, but it was far from "mission accomplished." We had no scholarships or financial sponsorship, so for Jan to continue on as a student, we had to earn enough money to support ourselves.

For me, it was in some respects a bittersweet time. It was wonderful to be so close to such a thriving, energetic campus and to be involved in many aspects of student life. And yet, as a nonstudent, I was ultimately on the outside, looking in. I longed to study and I drank in the books Jan brought home and constantly asked him to tell me about his classes. But we could only afford for one of us to study and we'd decided that Jan would study first and I'd get my opportunity later.

A New Normal

Jan had found work as a hospital orderly in the nearby town of St. Joseph. It was a pleasant, well-run hospital that catered largely to comfortably off patients—those who could afford medical insurance.

Before I'd arrived, Jan had asked around about work opportunities for me and had arranged for me to interview at the nearby Berrien County Hospital. This hospital served mainly migrant workers who flocked to Michigan as seasonal pickers of berries, asparagus, and other crops. A Norwegian girl had worked there previously and had apparently done a good job, so my nationality worked in my favor. The hospital was woefully short of trained nursing staff and I was told I'd be given three months' training and then would be in "charge" of the eight-patient obstetrics ward from 3:00–11:00 P.M. each day. The training would consist of basic nursing skills and at the end of it I'd be expected to care for my patients alone, although the paperwork would be signed by the nurse in charge on the internal medicine ward on the floor below.

One of my first patients during this training period was a lady in a coma. Every time I entered her room, I cast a horrified glance at the Roman Catholic crucifix that lay against her chest. As someone born and raised in Lutheran Norway, this symbol of Catholicism inspired a depth of fear and revulsion in me for which I have no rational explanation.

Today, whenever I feel frustrated with someone who I feel is being narrow-minded, judgmental, or prejudiced, I think back to my unreasonable fear of this poor Catholic lady.

I remind myself that we're each at a different point on our cultural and spiritual journey and that God, in His time, will lead us to where He wants us to be.

My English skills, or lack thereof, added another layer of "adventure" to my training at the hospital. One of my regular tasks was to check the BPR—blood pressure, pulse, and respiration—of a very ill lady on the medical ward. One day, I noticed she wasn't on my list and I asked an orderly why she'd been crossed off.

"Oh, she kicked the bucket," he said casually. He was using an

American expression for death that I'd never before encountered.

I looked at him in disbelief. "No, no, that can't be true," I said. "She is far too sick for anything like that!" He laughed and laughed, and soon my comment was providing amusement for the rest of the nursing staff as well. In fact, for those first few weeks, almost anything I said seemed to provoke laughter.

Shortly after I'd joined Jan in America, he'd suggested we stop speaking Norwegian altogether. English was the "official" language of the Adventist Church, he argued, and disciplining ourselves to speak it all the time would go a long way toward improving our skills. Jan also believed that constantly referring to a dictionary to search out the best English word would "slow us down." Instead, he advised me to "read everything you can—books, magazines, newspapers." So I read widely and labored each day over the newspaper and, sure enough, my English language vocabulary began to expand.

Unfortunately, I still sometimes deployed my newly acquired words in novel ways. During my three-month training period at the hospital, I worked in central supply, sterilizing, wrapping, and labeling medical instruments for later use. I also sometimes worked in the operating theater where my task was to find instruments as they were needed, and read out the name of each item before handing it over to be used.

One day an appendectomy was on the schedule. I found a requested instrument and confidently read out the label I'd written on the outside of the package. "Rape retractor," I announced.

There was a moment's silence as my words sank in, and then—much to my confusion—the theater staff burst into laughter. Later, my supervisor kindly explained to me my one-letter mistake: the correct name for the instrument was "rake retractor." My diligent reading of the newspaper—especially the crime section—had probably helped bring the wrong word to my mind.

My English quickly improved but my time at the hospital proved to be a continual learning experience. Up until that time, I'd never met anyone who was illiterate, yet so many of those I served couldn't read or even write their own name. I encountered, also, so many patients with venereal diseases. I remember pretty young girls—barely out of puberty—whose already grim prospects in life had been blighted further by a sexually transmitted disease or an unwanted pregnancy. In fact, a majority of those in our maternity ward were unmarried. This was a face of America that I hadn't expected and I was profoundly disturbed. For a time, I felt that Jan and I had come to a God-forsaken country.

As we settled into life in Berrien Springs, there was a great sense of accomplishment. Together, we'd faced down financial challenges and language barriers, and we'd adapted to this new, alien culture. We'd learned new skills and made many new friends. The multicultural milieu on campus added to our sense that we were part of a great global mission movement and it was an exhilarating feeling.

In the midst of our busy schedules, we occasionally found time to just enjoy being a newly married couple. We'd discovered the joys of the American game of "mini-golf" and these excursions together were our special treat.

Yet there were times, also, when I felt a sneaking sense of disappointment. I felt let down when I met students who thought nothing of attending the cinema, or whose way of keeping the Sabbath seemed so odd to my eyes. Sometimes I felt terribly ignorant and backward—out of step with these young American Adventists. At other times, I simply felt judged, as if my "brand" of Adventism was perceived as less than it should be.

Between work and school, Jan survived on a minimum of sleep. I'll never understand how he managed to keep up with his studies, let alone earn good grades as well. At the end of his second year at EMC, he'd finished his bachelor's degree and we were ready to move on to the next stage of our adventure.

Chapter 9

A Balancing Act

T O THE MODERN EAR, ELIJAH'S words to God in 1 Kings 19:4 have an all-too-familiar ring.

"I've had enough, Lord," he says. He's depleted every last bit of energy and self-discipline in facing down the priests of Baal on Mount Carmel and fleeing the wrath of Queen Jezebel, and now he wants God to know that he's done. He's reached his breaking point. He has nothing left to give.

Our daily stressors and energy drains are probably more mundane than pagan priests or murderous queens. But it's a rare person who can't relate to Elijah's heartfelt words.

"I've had enough, Lord."

I know from experience that the life of a minister—and that of his or her spouse—is often out of balance. There can be too much time spent with other people's problems, not enough dealing with our own. Too many weekend or evening events that eat away at time spent with family. There can be too few opportunities for the solitude we need to recharge our emotional and spiritual batteries.

It's not just clergy and their families who need to take care on this point. Our enthusiasm for the Lord's work can sometimes mean we shortchange our families, ourselves, and ironically, even our God.

I find it very telling that when God begins to address Elijah's exhaustion (1 Kings 19:5–9), He starts with the absolute basics—food and rest. It's an incredibly revealing moment: God, the Father, dealing with His tired, cranky child. It reminds me a little of when a baby cries and we instinctively begin running through a mental checklist.

A Balancing Act

Is she hungry? Does she need to be changed? Is she overdue on her nap?

Making the effort to take proper care of ourselves isn't a luxury—it's good stewardship of our God-given resources. I've lived with a chronic disease for more than forty years and I'm well acquainted with the relationship between exhaustion and all our other physical and emotional systems—and, yes, even our spiritual equilibrium.

In the midst of any dark night of the soul, I've found that it's wise to do a quick top-to-toe physical evaluation. Have I been eating well? Have I been keeping up with exercise, even if it's just a quick walk around the block? Am I getting regular, good-quality time with my family and social support network? Sometimes the problem needn't become a full-blown spiritual or emotional crisis. Sometimes we just need more sleep.

As young people, anxious to finish study and join "God's workforce," Jan and I sometimes pushed our physical limits. We were soon to discover that this sort of haste comes with certain costs.

Our experience, though, is far from unique. I suspect that balance remains an elusive goal for many of us as we try to control the multiplying demands on our time and energy.

I believe this problem can be especially acute within families of church workers, or those who carry many responsibilities within the local church. Somehow, it just doesn't feel right to say "No" to God's work, and so we keep saying "Yes" even if our family life or personal health suffers.

We don't lack for information about how to live a balanced life. The wholistic message of our Adventist faith clearly reveals the interconnected nature of our physical, emotional, and spiritual systems. Many years ago, Ellen White wrote, "Temperance in all things . . . in eating, drinking, sleeping . . . is one of the grand principles of the religious life."* She knew that caring for our own basic human needs was a prerequisite for being effective workers for God. Many times, she warned that even those who labor for Christ would be

---

* *Testimonies for the Church,* (1900) 6:375.

better to "leave undone some of the things planned for the day's work than to undo oneself and become overtaxed . . ."*

Yes, we know the importance of proper rest, physical care, and spiritual nourishment. Yet, who among us actually manages to put what we know into regular practice? How often do we become "undone" by allowing ourselves to be worn down by the stresses and demands of life?

Perhaps it would be better if we didn't think of "balance" as an end point that we'll one day reach. Our striving to reach this magical state—when everything we are trying to juggle actually stays up in the air—is probably just another stress we can do without!

No, I don't think balance is a destination so much as a way of thinking that we try to weave into our everyday decision-making. Rather than a state of zenlike equilibrium, I think balance means the ability to accept that life is messy and that we won't achieve everything we set out to accomplish each day. It means prioritizing and taking care of the basics. At times, it can mean having the courage to "leave undone some of the things planned for the day's work." And perhaps it also means confessing to God, in the words of Elijah, that sometimes we've just "had enough" and we need His help.

Takoma Park

When Jan and I moved from Michigan to Takoma Park, Maryland, in 1957, we were curious to experience this place that was widely known as the epicenter of global Adventism. In the 1950s, this suburb of Washington, D.C., just six miles from the White House, was a leafy green oasis, slightly elevated from the surrounding city, and known for the clear spring water of Sligo Creek. It still retained the feel of a village, and its character and rhythms were shaped in large part by the many Adventist institutions it hosted.

There was the General Conference headquarters on the corner of Eastern Avenue and Willow Street, and the Review and Herald Publishing House on Laurel Street. A little farther away, the

---

* *Mind, Character, and Personality*, (1903) 2:375, 376.

A Balancing Act

Washington Sanitarium and Washington Missionary College dominated a forty-eight-acre parcel of land on the banks of Sligo Creek. There was the J. N. Andrews School on Elm Avenue and the large Sligo Church on Flower Ave. There was also Takoma Park Church, the Columbia Union Conference headquarters, Takoma Academy, the Home Study Institute, an Adventist Book Center, and a smattering of other church-related buildings and enterprises scattered throughout the town. At the time, it was estimated that almost one-third of the residents of Takoma Park were church members and many were in church employ or attending church-run schools.

Our interest, of course, was centered on the Adventist Theological Seminary, located next to the General Conference headquarters and behind the publishing house, where Jan had enrolled to complete a master's program.

Jan soon found work as a night watchman and janitor at the General Conference. He had no choice but to work to help pay living expenses and tuition, and he was thankful to have the job, but his schedule was less than sane. He came home every morning from his overnight shift, more asleep than awake, and fell into bed for two hours. The rest of the day was devoted to classes and study, although he managed to catch another two hours of sleep in the early evening by sleeping on a sofa in the General Conference before his night shift began.

Following our move to Maryland, our personal finances were in poor shape, so I was determined to find a higher paying job than I'd had in Michigan. Now that my English was passable, I felt confident enough to go to an employment agency and look for office work.

One of the first interviews I attended was with a bank. From the moment I walked up the stairs and through the front doors, I knew I wanted to work there—its quiet lobby was a far cry from the shabby wards and overworked staff of the county hospital in Michigan. And the salary was excellent!

The interview went well, the manager chatted to me pleasantly, and my hopes rose. As the interview was winding up, he looked down briefly at my résumé and said, "Mrs. Paulsen, I see here that you are a Seventh-day Adventist. What kind are you?"

For a moment, I wondered if my English had failed me. What kind of Adventist was I?

"Sir, I'm not sure what you mean," I said.

"Well, I've employed a number of Adventists through the years, and some of them want to go home early on Fridays and won't work on Saturdays. There are sometimes busy periods here at the bank when all my staff must pitch in and work weekends. Could you do that?"

"Oh, I can definitely work Sundays," I said. "But I can't work after sundown Friday or on Saturday."

He looked at me for a long moment and said, "Well, Mrs. Paulsen, you had the job, but now I don't have any choice. We can't hire you."

I was heartbroken but I kept searching. Finally, I found a job at an insurance agency in Washington, D.C., close to the Library of Congress on Independence Ave. Every morning I took a half-hour bus trip from Takoma Park, eyes glued to the window, as we wended down through the suburbs of Washington, past the gleaming marble edifice of the U. S. Capitol Building, past the monuments and green expanse of the National Mall, to my downtown office.

Returning home

The year prior to moving to Takoma Park, Jan and I had put our names down for a seminary apartment, but there was none to be had. Instead, we found a basement apartment one street away from Sligo Church. Our new home had windows that opened directly onto the pavement parallel to our apartment. Our "view" consisted of frequent below-the-knee glimpses of passing pedestrians.

These windows had very flimsy locks and each evening, with Jan working security at the General Conference, I cowered under the bed covers, praying that no one would open the windows and crawl through. But this wasn't the worst feature of our new home. It was terribly hot. There were a series of heating pipes in the roof above us, and these, combined with the heat of a Maryland summer, made our rooms stifling. Not a breath of fresh air seemed to disturb the sticky heat inside.

We began searching for different accommodation and in the winter we moved into a small attic apartment and immediately proceeded to freeze. I think the hardship probably seems greater in hindsight, for I don't recall feeling any great dissatisfaction at the time! Jan and I counted ourselves immensely fortunate for the opportunities we were enjoying.

We were living in the United States, however, on borrowed time. Each year, we had to receive permission from church leaders in our home territory—the West Nordic Union—to continue study, even though the union wasn't supporting us financially. We'd made a commitment to return to ministry in Norway, and by the end of the 1959 school year, we felt it was now time to go back. Jan had only one year left to complete his bachelor of divinity degree, and we were determined that we'd eventually come back to America for that final year of study.

We sold some belongings, packed up the rest, and booked our passage back to Norway. But before we left America, we applied for a re-entry visa that would give me a two-year window of time in which to return. Jan was on a student visa.

Back in Norway, Jan launched himself wholeheartedly into pastoral ministry at the *Adventkirken* in Arendal, an historic coastal town in the southern part of the country. I found part-time work at a local hospital, and returned to canvassing part-time. In my "spare time," I took classes in accounting and business law at a nearby business college. Between us, we managed to cover our living expenses and keep our little Volkswagen Beetle running, but that was about all.

We soon settled into a routine—me with work and study, and Jan enjoying his transition from the classroom to active ministry. But there were occasional bumps along the way.

"Kari, why aren't you in class on Saturdays?" asked one of my instructors at the business college. I explained that Saturday was my Sabbath day of rest, but he was unmoved. "If you don't attend, there's no way you'll be able to keep up with the rest of the class," he declared. I determined to prove him wrong, and I did.

Against All Odds

A new arrival

Laila Paulsen was born into our family on February 15, 1961—a beautiful little baby girl who added a whole new dimension of joy to our lives. Towards the end of my pregnancy, I was monitored for Rhesus incompatibility. In very simple terms, it's a condition where antibodies in a pregnant woman's blood destroy her baby's blood cells. It only happens when the mother has rhesus-negative blood (RhD negative) and her baby has rhesus-positive blood (RhD positive). There's another factor too—the mother must also have been previously sensitized to RhD-positive blood. For me, this had happened more than a decade earlier during my recovery from heart surgery when I'd received transfusions of incompatible blood.

Today, Rh incompatibility can easily be prevented in pregnancy with a series of injections. But in Laila's time, the only available treatment was to induce delivery early and then sometimes withdraw most of the baby's own blood, bit by bit, replacing it with fresh blood.

Back to Michigan

Since returning to Norway, we hadn't given up our plan to return to the United States for Jan to complete his one year bachelor of divinity at the Theological Seminary—which had since been moved from Takoma Park to Emmanuel Missionary College (later Andrews University). In May 1961, just a few months after Laila's birth, we sold our furniture and our car for our fares back to Michigan.

Jan would first be attending summer school to get a head start on Hebrew exegesis—a subject he hadn't studied for eight years. For these few weeks, he didn't intend to work so he could focus on what he anticipated would be a difficult subject.

But no sooner than we arrived in Berrien Springs than Jan received a phone call from the head nurse at the hospital where he'd once worked as an orderly.

"Paulsen, I heard you're back again," she said, with her usual brisk manner. "I'm in desperate need for someone to look after a private patient. He's not going to live long, but I need someone to be with him for the twelve-hour night shift, seven days a week."

"I'm not so sure I can do that," said Jan. "I'm in full-time studies."

"But it's probably not going to be for long," she said. "We really don't think he has much time left to live. Plus, it's a well-paid position. Can't you at least start and see how it goes?"

As usual, we weren't swimming in money so, with many misgivings, Jan took the job. But his patient obviously hadn't heard the dire predictions about his own death. He lived and showed every sign of continuing to do so.

Before long, Jan was back into his old routine of catching two hours of sleep in the morning, attending classes, then getting another two hours of sleep in the evening before heading out to work. There were exams looming in a few weeks, and I said, "Jan, this isn't going to work—you just can't go on like this." I found a babysitter for Laila, a wonderful South African lady, and I went out to look for work.

I soon found a bookkeeping position with a company in nearby Benton Harbor that dealt in wholesale appliances, but Jan continued on with his night job—he felt duty bound to stay with his patient until another caretaker could be found. For the next few weeks, we rarely saw each other. Our paths would cross between seven and eight o'clock each morning, as I was going out to work and he was arriving home.

On the morning of his final exam, I thought that Jan was looking very pale.

"Are you going to get any sleep today?" I asked him.

"Of course!" he said. "I'll sleep after I've finished my exam." What he failed to mention, however, was that he'd not had any sleep for the past two days. He'd been too busy studying. His philosophy was basically, "I'm healthy, I'm strong; I can do anything if I put my mind to it. Mind over matter!"

He went and took his exam and then came home and fell into bed. He awoke soon after to the sound of a violent summer storm outside and with a sinking feeling, he remembered that he'd left a window down in the car. He dragged himself out of bed, went downstairs, and closed the car window, walked back inside the apartment and promptly passed out. I found him hours later when I got home from work.

In recent years, doctors have offered various explanations for what probably happened to Jan that day. Yet at the time, the physicians who treated him were uncertain what had caused his body to seemingly "shut down." Did fatigue play a role—his months of very little sleep and overexertion? Well, at the very least, I'm sure it didn't help!

For two days, Jan remained in the hospital in a deep coma. His doctor decided not to give Jan fluids through an intravenous line in case he had a brain tumor—if this was the case, they didn't want to increase the pressure on his brain. But for a six-foot four-inch man to be without fluids for that long in the summer heat was a serious matter.

Finally, the doctor told me that Jan must be transferred to the neurological unit in South Bend, Indiana, and he arranged for Jan to make the hour-long journey by ambulance.

What I didn't realize at the time was that Jan's medical insurance (which we had through the college) was only valid during official school semesters. Thus, the expense of the medical treatment Jan was receiving, as well as the ambulance trip, would be our responsibility.

"So long as he's alive!"

In South Bend, I continued sitting by Jan's bed, praying for some sign of life. The neurosurgeon wasn't encouraging. "Kari, are Jan's parent's alive?" he asked. I nodded. "Well, it's time to call them. I don't hold out much hope."

After a pause, he added, "Mrs. Paulsen, even if he does come out of his coma, you're going to have to face the very real possibility that your husband may have sustained some brain damage."

During all this time, we had a legion of fellow students and faculty praying for Jan's recovery. Michigan camp meeting was also in full swing at the time, and a special season of prayer was held there for Jan.

On the afternoon of the third day of Jan's coma, the wife of one of the seminary professors—a lovely Norwegian lady—came to the hospital. She said, "Kari, you have to eat; you can't go on like this. And remember, you have a little girl to care for too." Over my protests, she took me to the restaurant of a nearby Howard Johnson motel.

And I did eat. She ordered a plate of French fries for me, which she knew I loved, and I remember sitting there with her, dipping the fries in ketchup.

When we returned to the hospital, all the nurses I encountered were smiling broadly. "He's woken up!" said one. I wanted so much to rush straight to his room, but I was made to stay outside until the doctor could thoroughly examine him. The wait was interminable. I sat and stared at the walls of the waiting area as different scenarios played through my mind. Would there be permanent damage? If so, what were we to do?

The doctor, when he finally came out to me, was smiling. "Mrs. Paulsen, you have a very intelligent husband."

"I don't care, just so long as he's alive," I said, and started crying violently. The tension of the past few days had built up inside me to an almost unbearable level, and now it overflowed.

Jan was terribly weak, but the doctor assured him that he'd been "very lucky" to escape any long-term physical or mental damage. Jan and I were convinced, of course, that it wasn't luck, but the power of prayer.

Jan was discharged the following day because we couldn't afford to let our medical bills pile up any higher. A kind Norwegian couple invited us to live with them for a transition period until we could get back on our feet. Soon, the fall term resumed and Jan began attending classes and studying, Laila went to her babysitter, and I went out to work. But it was two or three months before Jan was himself again—the incident had taken a tremendous toll on him.

Curiously, for the remainder of the school year, a large carton of groceries appeared every Friday at our front door. We've never been able to discover who took it upon themselves to do this and they'll never know how immensely helpful, and appreciated, their kindness was.

Against All Odds

When Jan graduated, we were approached about various ministerial positions. There was one in Minnesota, and one in California—both of which were initially very tempting to us. And then there came a call for Jan to go to a small teacher training school in Ghana, Africa, to be a Bible teacher and the campus pastor.

Jan and I scarcely needed to discuss it. When the call from Africa came, we said to each other, "This is what we should do." God, in His mercy, had given Jan a fresh chance at life, and the most important question for us was, "Where can we best serve Him?"

The answer, it seemed, was the hot, dusty, equatorial town of Bekwai in central Ghana—a place almost beyond the imagination of two Norwegians who were infinitely more familiar with snow and ice.

Chapter 10

Turning Point

THERE'S A WHOLE FIELD OF psychological research called "life course theory" and a central concept in this is the idea of "turning points."

Psychologists study how early life events or circumstances contribute to later life choices. They ask: How are turning points such as marriage, divorce, health choices, career choices, or all manner of other variables, related to the course of our future life?

It reminds me of the once-popular series of children's books called *Choose Your Own Adventure*. The reader herself becomes the main character, and as the plot unfolds, you're presented with various choices at key moments. The choices you make lead you, step by step, through the book toward either a happy or tragic ending.

However, it seems to me that apart from obvious choices such as our marriage partner or career, and the like, major turning points in our lives aren't always immediately discernable. It's only later, as we look back, that many of the pivotal moments in our life's journey take on an extra clarity and we can say with any measure of certainty, "Yes, *that* was a turn in my path that has brought me to where I am today"; or "It was *that* moment where it could have gone either way."

Sometimes the most profound turning points come wrapped up in the mundane of everyday routine. And sometimes, they're not really sharp, 90-degree turning points, but rather a long, very gradual change in direction.

Against All Odds

Was Moses, tending his father-in-law's flocks of sheep, aware that his forty-year sojourn in the wilderness of Midian was just a long, drawn-out turning point in his life? Could the fisherman Simon Peter have foreseen, as he was invited into Jesus' entourage, that it would eventually take him from the lakeside of Galilee, to a martyr's death in a foreign land?

Mark Twain, in the very last essay he wrote for publication, satirized the extent we believe specific events or choices impact our life's course. His article, "The Turning Point of My Life," was commissioned in 1909 by *Harper's Bazaar* magazine. In it, he wrote that what we perceive as major life turning points are usually "only the *last* link in a very long chain of turning-points . . . [and] not any more important than the humblest of its ten thousand predecessors."*

I tend to agree. The way we choose to live every day impacts our life's course, just as much as the major decisions we make. And it's only later that the cumulative impact of our choices—large and small—become apparent.

This is especially true for young people, although during this period of our lives, we're often oblivious to the tremendous power of our choices. During our teens, as we're experimenting with independence—trying on different ideas and identities—our future so often hangs in the balance, and yet we have no sense of the import of seemingly minor decisions. What we read, who we spend our time with, what we watch, where we go; all these little choices add up and inevitably push us toward one path or another.

Looking back, it's clear that our decision to accept a mission call to Ghana was a turning point for us, but not quite in the sense we were expecting at the time. We went to Ghana with the intent of making a difference in others' lives through our mission service, but I suspect the lives that were changed most radically were our own.

My husband, Jan, has often said that when we entered Africa, Africa entered us. And it's true. Our years in Ghana and Nigeria changed us radically and permanently. We grew up; we were thrust

---

* Seymour Barofsky, ed., *The Wisdom of Mark Twain* (New York: Citadel Press, 2003), 57.

into situations that were well and truly outside our experience, and sometimes probably outside our competence. We encountered cultural realities that forced us to think outside the relatively narrow Western worldview that had thus far been our guide.

Spiritually, we learned that relying on God was far more than just an abstract ideal—it became a day-by-day, sometimes moment-by-moment necessity.

Africa also left another permanent mark on me—a physical mark; one that I struggle with, even today.

Yet, at the time, we had no clue that our time in Africa would have such an impact on our future. We were just a young family, far from home, ready for adventure, and filled with a tremendous sense of gratitude that, finally, we'd be getting a "walk-on" part in God's grand mission drama.

Bekwai

When I picture our home in Bekwai, Ghana, I see red dirt. Clouds of red dirt kicked up by children playing or by a passing pickup truck. Red dirt clinging to your clothes and skin. Red dirt glowing gold in the evening.

In writing about our time in Ghana, I'm very conscious that I'm writing about a time and place that is, in many ways, removed from the Ghana of today. My memories belong to a specific time in the history of that country, when it was still emerging from the shadows of colonialism and grappling with many related political and developmental challenges. In the fifty years that have passed, internal changes as well as the forces of globalism have altered the cultural and political landscape of Ghana, and I suspect if I returned today I'd see only hints of the Ghana of my memories.

The Bekwai we came to in the mid-1960s was a small town some 150 miles north of the Ghanaian capital Accra, and it had a real frontier feel. There were clay and sheet metal huts and buildings, a bustling outside marketplace, and the deep green of tropical foliage all around. And it was *hot*.

The Adventist secondary school and teachers' training college where Jan would teach had been established just over a decade earlier, and with some four hundred students enrolled, it was a hive of energy and activity. It was located on a hilltop, about a mile north of the center of town.

When we arrived, we discovered that little house we'd been assigned on the edge of the campus was already occupied—with vermin of many different shapes and sizes. Among the most persistent were the cockroaches; they were large, black, and tenacious. No matter what tactic we used to try and get rid of them, they seemed to delight in turning up again soon afterward, as if telling us *we* were the intruders, not them. In the end, we simply placed the four legs of our food cupboard in water-filled tins in an effort to stop the cockroaches' picnicking activities.

Jan and I, along with one-and-a-half-year-old Laila, had traveled to Bekwai with all our belongings packed into two large drums. Before we left the United States, we'd been given a missionary's "outfitting allowance" to buy necessities for our new mission posting. We'd used the money, instead, to pay off our hospital debt from Jan's recent illness. In a way, it was good for us. Instead of trying to import Western comforts into Africa, we were forced to live more like our local Ghanaian neighbors and to buy food and clothes in the nearby market. We didn't feel poor; we felt like we "fitted in."

The campus had only intermittent electricity. The generator was put on each Sunday for a few hours so we could do some washing, but during the week we relied on kerosene for lighting, and for refrigerating our food, and gas for cooking. All our water had to be boiled for twenty minutes and then filtered. We soaked our fruit and vegetables in Milton, a chlorine bleach solution, or potassium permanganate, if the produce had a thick, peelable skin.

I bought yam, cassava, and unrefined rice at the market. If we were lucky, we could sometimes buy carrots or potatoes that had been grown in northern Ghana and trucked down to Kumasi.

Before we'd left the United States, we'd made careful inquiries about local hospitals. Since Laila's birth and the trauma she'd endured with my Rhesus factor problems, we knew that any children we had in the future could require a complete blood change-over immediately following birth and would always need to be induced early.

We'd been assured there was a good Adventist hospital just an hour's drive from Bekwai. Soon after arriving in Ghana, I became pregnant and we traveled to this hospital to talk with the doctor there. Even before we walked through the doors, we began to suspect this mission hospital wouldn't be able to provide the care we needed.

The doctor confirmed this, saying, "No, we can't change blood here, but I'll send you down to the capital, Accra, to the military hospital there."

So we made the five-hour trip south to Accra to see the British-trained doctor at the military hospital.

"Oh, I've done this procedure many times in England," he said. "But we can't do it here—we don't have a properly screened blood supply. It would be best for you to leave Africa to have your baby."

It was a serious blow to us, but we had no choice. When I was seven months pregnant, Laila and I traveled to Oslo, Norway.

Laila had turned two a few months earlier and she didn't speak any Norwegian. She understood Afrikaans (the mother tongue of her babysitter in Michigan), along with English, and some words in the local Ghanaian dialects. When we arrived in Oslo, I would be going straight into the hospital and Laila would go home with my family. She was so young and vulnerable, and would feel so isolated and frightened among these Norwegian-speaking strangers. I fretted the whole trip. How could I let her go? What choice did I have? It was heartbreaking to part with her and leave her in the care of my mother and sisters.

I was in my seventh month of pregnancy but I had only gained three pounds. After I'd been admitted to the hospital in Oslo, I was started on a high-calorie diet, which I involuntarily thwarted by being violently sick. When I was eight months along, the doctors decided the bilirubin level had climbed too high for the safety of the baby, so they induced labor.

Against All Odds

Jan Rune was born four weeks early after a two-and-a-half hour labor. He was transferred to the children's hospital and seemed to respond well to treatment. After several days, he was brought back to me at the women's hospital and I began nursing him, but within hours he suffered a relapse. His bilirubin levels shot up and the doctors again began treatment. Medical science has since discovered that the first milk produced by mothers with Rhesus factor issues contains a concentration of harmful antibodies and should never be given to the baby. At the time, however, the doctors were mystified by Jan Rune's setback.

I stayed in Norway following Jan Rune's birth until his doctor gave him a medical "all-clear." I couldn't wait for our family to be back together again, and I wrote to Jan telling him we'd soon be back home in Ghana and giving him my flight arrival information.

Unfortunately, I didn't realize that the church division headquarters in England also needed to sign off on my clearance to return to Africa. On the Sabbath before we were due to fly out, someone from the local church union office called me aside.

"Mrs. Paulsen, you can't leave tomorrow," he told me. "I know you have your tickets and all the arrangements are made, but you can't leave until your doctor in Oslo has signed the medical clearance papers that the division office has sent."

It was the weekend, and my doctor at the hospital was not on duty and couldn't be contacted. A church union official spent Sunday morning on the phone trying to get permission from the division office in England to allow me to fly. I packed my suitcases and went to the airport with Jan Rune and Laila, waiting to hear whether I'd be able to board the plane. No permission came, and we missed our flight.

We were able to reschedule our flights for a few days later, but there was another problem: How could we let Jan know about our change in plans? He had already traveled down to Accra to meet us, and the church office there was closed for the weekend. There was no way to get a message through.

Jan met the plane we were due to arrive on, eager to see his family and meet his new son. We weren't on board the flight. Anxiously, he quizzed the airport staff. They contacted the airline staff in Oslo, who said, "Well, we believe she got on the plane in Norway, but somewhere in between a connecting flight in Europe we lost track of her."

He was beside himself. What had happened to his wife, his newborn baby, and his two-and-a-half-year-old daughter? It wasn't until Tuesday that someone from Norway finally managed to get a message through to Jan via the church union office in Accra.

Malaria

After returning home to Bekwai from Norway, I kept busy caring for Jan Rune and Laila, and started to get back into the rhythm of campus life. But when Jan Rune was just eight months old, something happened that irrevocably changed my future course. Jan and I didn't know it then, but in hindsight, it was an event that would always mark a "before" and "after" point in our lives.

I got malaria. This in itself was somewhat unremarkable as both Jan and I had already come down with malarial fever during the time we'd been in Ghana. It was difficult to avoid—the prophylactic we were taking was not 100 percent effective. Whenever we felt the telltale signs of fever, we'd start doses of Camaquine or Chloroquine, and after a time the fever always broke and we mended. But this time was different.

Jan was away in Nigeria, conducting a week of prayer series at an Adventist secondary school. Early one morning I felt the signs of fever and I immediately began the proper medications. My fever quickly climbed past 103 degrees and I began to suspect there was something very wrong, indeed.

Since coming to Bekwai we'd had a Muslim "house boy" named Tinga. We soon learned not to judge him by his tattered clothing. He was hardworking, a quick learner, and very kind. Most of the money he earned went straight back to his home village to help support his extended family. He'd worked for another missionary family and had learned to make the best bread and the most delicious gluten. We also had a part-time helper named Benjamin—an Adventist student who came to cook and help out around the house for two hours a day.

As my fever mounted I grew increasingly disorientated, and I called out to Benjamin.

"Benjamin, get someone. I'm not well."

Within minutes, he had brought help back to me. The wife of the secondary school headmaster took Jan Rune to care for him. Laila and I were moved to the home of the principal of the teacher training college. I was still conscious by the time a local doctor arrived to look at me. She was a recent medical graduate from Europe and she'd only just arrived in Ghana. Her experience with malaria, beyond what she'd learned from textbooks, was minimal. She gave me an injection of what we later discovered was a huge dose of Nivaquine, a form of chloroquine sulphate. Her "mistake" probably kept me alive, for what I had was a virulent form of cerebral malaria. The injection saved my life, but the megadose I received ultimately led to an almost complete loss of hearing in my left ear, along with a permanent tinnitus, or ringing sensation.

The doctor left. The last thing I remember before I lost consciousness was a need to visit the bathroom. I toppled from the bed and crawled across the floor toward the door. And I don't remember anything else.

When I began to emerge from my coma, my first impressions were hazy. I was in a bed with many other people around me. It was hot. It was noisy. I could make out the white, gauzy film of a mosquito net surrounding my bed. There was an IV line in my arm. I felt an overwhelming thirst.

I was in the hospital at Kumasi, some twenty-five miles north of Bekwai, and I had been unconscious for three days. Gradually, my moments of awareness grew longer and my perceptions sharper. I noticed a nurse changing the dressing of the patient in the bed next to mine. The patient had a large suppurating topical ulcer on her leg. Queasily, I watched the nurse clean the weeping wound with her ungloved hands.

Turning Point

I called weakly to her. "Can I have some water?"

She turned and pointed to a thermos on my nightstand.

"There's some water," she said.

"Is it cold?" I asked.

"Yes, I think it's cold," she said. "Let me check."

She unscrewed the lid of the thermos and touched the water with the tip of her finger.

Without warning, I vomited.

I'm going to die here, I thought as I drifted in and out of consciousness.

Kumasi Hospital was a state-run facility that provided medical care to surrounding communities, dispensing life-saving medicines and treatments that wouldn't otherwise have been available. Yet this was Ghana of fifty years ago, and my experiences at this hospital no doubt reflected many of the challenges of that era—not least, finding enough trained nursing staff.

Later, I became aware that a hospital orderly was moving my bed and wheeling me down a hallway. He took me down to the laboratory to have my blood drawn. I lay on my bed, at face-level with a long, wooden counter stained with countless blood spills. A nurse applied a tourniquet to my arm and started searching for a productive vein. She stuck in the needle, but no blood flowed into the syringe. Frustrated, she pulled the needle out and lay it down on that hideous, blood-stained wooden counter, then tried again. I vomited.

Salt!

The staff at Bekwai school had managed to get a message to Jan and he cut short his visit in Nigeria and came straight to Kumasi. The medical staff at the hospital told him it was too early to discharge me, but I begged him to take me home.

"Jan, you've got to get me out of here," I said. "Perhaps the malaria will kill me, but if I stay here for too much longer, it will *definitely* kill me."

So Jan took me home. For days, I was so sick; I vomited and vomited. My blood pressure dropped alarmingly. My illness had long since ceased following the typical course of malaria and I soon developed a terrible hunger for salt. At times, I thought I could do almost anything just to feel the taste of salt on my tongue. My body craved salt, and unknown to me, it needed this salt to survive.

In Norway, I had grown up eating salted herring, and the thought of this started to become an obsession with me.

If I could just have some of that salted herring, I thought, *I'd soon be myself again.*

For the next few months, our family struggled on; Jan taught his classes and got on with his duties at the school, all while looking after me and the children as well.

Tinga, our houseboy, was a mainstay. He told me that he had fasted and prayed to Allah for the three days I'd been in a coma. As extra "insurance" he'd also sacrificed a chicken to his ancestral gods. Either way, he was convinced his piety had contributed greatly to my survival, and we loved him for his compassion.

After a few months, I started to feel a little better, but my craving for salt continued. We had a lemon orchard near our house and I went through half a bucket of lemons each week. I'd squeeze a lemon and add enough salt to make a thick paste and eat it with a spoon. It was heaven. Of course, it was a guilty pleasure. Everything I'd learned about the principles of healthy living told me that excess salt had no place in a "good Adventist's" diet. So, I ate my salt paste in the kitchen, where no one could see me and this literally kept me alive.

One day, I suddenly felt better. I started to feel more like myself again. Relieved, Jan and I felt that this particular saga was finally drawing to a long-overdue close. I'm glad we had no way of knowing that it was really just beginning.

Nigeria

As my strength started to return, we were dealt another surprise—this time, a happy one. Jan received a call to move to Nigeria to the Seventh-day Adventist college at Ilishan-Remo, an hour's drive north from the capital, Lagos. He would be registrar and Bible teacher (later president) at this new institution—the Adventist College of West Africa, now known as Babcock University. It was the kind of challenge he relished, and we began to shake off the traumas of the past year and look to the road ahead.

Chapter 11
Trustworthy and True

NINETEENTH CENTURY RUSSIAN AUTHOR FYODOR Dostoyevsky had a gift for bringing heartbreak to life though words on the page. So many of the dramatic themes in his novels revolve around the darker human experiences—inexplicable misfortune, emotional and physical suffering, guilt. His own experiences go some way, perhaps, to explaining his focus on these more melancholic themes. In 1849, Dostoyevsky's life abruptly changed course when he was arrested for alleged political conspiracy and sentenced to death. At the very last moment, while he stood blindfolded in front of a firing squad, a note from Tsar Nicholas I arrived commuting Dostoyevsky's sentence to four years in Siberia with hard labor. It's probably not terribly surprising that his subsequent books tend to plumb the depth of human cruelty and suffering. Lighthearted reading they are not!

Yet what makes Dostoyevsky's writing so compelling and so enduring is that he taps into a stream of human emotion that is common to each one of us at various points in our lives. We all suffer loss—and sometimes that loss is not just physical but intangible; things such as our hopes and dreams.

In *White Nights*, Dostoyevsky writes about the death of idealism. "[I]n vain does the dreamer rummage about in his old dreams, raking them over as though they were a heap of cinders, looking in these cinders for some spark, however tiny, to fan it into a flame so as to warm his chilled blood . . ."*

---

* Fyodor Dostoevsky, trans. David Magarshack, *Best Short Stories of Fyodor Dostoevsky* (New York: Random House, 1992), 28.

Sometimes it's not a pleasant experience to "rummage about in our old dreams." As children, the future stretches out before us, full of promise. As young people, our hopes for the future begin to take a more definite shape—in the form, perhaps, of a relationship, or a specific career, or a certain goal.

But then as we continue on through life, somewhere along the way we meet reality. Reality can come to us in the form of financial limitations or missed opportunities. Reality can erode our old dreams through the tedium of everyday routine, or through different responsibilities that seem as interminable as they are unavoidable. We meet reality when we come face to face with our own mortality through sickness or accident.

What happens when you and I rummage around in our old dreams and then hold them up to the light of our present day reality?

At that point, I believe, we have a choice. We can mourn the loss of "what could have been" and allow this to shape and define us—although this is a sure route toward cynicism, anger, and resentment.

What would happen, instead, if we chose to focus not on "might have been" but on what Christ says "*will* be." For me, this has been a lifeline in many, many difficult situations. Sometimes, there's just not a whole lot we can do about our derailed dreams. We can't go back into the past and make changes. We can't alter human nature—our own or others'. We can't singlehandedly rid the world of injustice or random tragedy.

But the certainty of ultimate renewal and restoration in Jesus Christ is a powerful antidote to disappointment. What our Lord offers us is not just "future tense." It's a process of renewal that begins today.

Through the years, I have found immense comfort in passages of Scripture that speak to this idea of restoration.

Paul writes, "The body that is sown is perishable, it is raised imperishable; it is sown in dishonor, it is raised in glory; it is sown in weakness, it is raised in power" (1 Corinthians 15:42, 43, NIV).

Or, in the words of John the revelator: "He who was seated on the throne said, 'I am making everything new!' Then he said, 'Write this down, for these words are trustworthy and true' " (Revelation 21:5, NIV).

The Lord may not necessarily dust off and revive all our old dreams or all the idealistic hopes we once had. But He can fill the space they've left behind with wonderful things, such as peace, security, and new dreams that are anchored in promises which are "trustworthy and true" and which will never "turn to cinder."

New lessons

The six years we spent in Africa were a time of incredible growth for us as a family, and for me personally. I had first left America for Ghana as a somewhat idealistic young woman. I was going to be a missionary! I was going to make a difference for God!

And that much was indeed true, but there was more to the story. The reality I found was more nuanced. In both Ghana and Nigeria, I soon discovered that my primary role was not "benefactor" but "student" and the reality I encountered taught me many things that have stayed with me through life.

I learned that poverty is a scourge that inflicts terrible scars on human beings; but I *also* learned that, in many situations, happiness has no relationship with material possessions.

I learned that my default cultural perspective is not necessarily the "neutral standard" by which I should judge others' customs and traditions.

I gained a completely new understanding of the importance of family ties and the interconnectedness of community life.

I learned that every dream I have for my life and for my family is contingent on factors that are outside my control, and that if you let it, this reality can crush your idealism and extinguish your faith.

But most importantly, I learned that when reality and idealism meet, the result doesn't have to be just the death of old dreams, but the birth of new ones.

Trustworthy and True

Water of life

We left Ghana in August 1964, and flew with Laila and Jan Rune almost six hundred miles east from Accra to Lagos, the capital city of Nigeria. The recently established Adventist College of West Africa was due to begin its new school year in September, so Jan was immediately absorbed by a myriad of challenges.

There were about ten to twelve other missionary families on campus, many with children, and Jan Rune and Laila were delighted to find so many new playmates. I reveled in the relatively reliable supply of electricity. It still came and went, but at least there tended to be more time with electricity than without. After using kerosene for so long to light our house and gas to cook our food, it was a novelty to be able to just flip a switch and to have the electricity work, at least most of the time. The local market had grains, yam, and cassava—food to which we'd long since grown accustomed.

What we didn't have in ready supply, however, was water, especially during the dry season, which lasted many months each year. Once a week, two staff members drove the college pickup truck into a nearby town and filled up large metal drums with water for the students and faculty. Each family was allocated a weekly supply of two drums and this water had to be used for everything—drinking, cooking, washing, and cleaning.

Jan Rune was in cloth diapers and keeping those clean with a limited water supply became an endless challenge. The trick was to set aside the week's drinking water, and then make sure you re-used every remaining drop of water multiple times.

You'd wash the dishes then ask yourself, "What can I use this water for next?" Maybe it could be used to clean or rinse dirty diapers.

There was no water for us to take proper baths. Instead, every day each family member was given a small basin of water for a sponge bath, and we became experts in the technique. At Christmastime, Jan would drive our family three hours up to the Ile-Ife Adventist Hospital and we'd stay there for a week. The highlight was being able to take three or four showers every day. What a luxury!

There was a wonderful spirit at the college. Our school

community worked, worshiped, and played together. Often on a Saturday night we'd meet at the homes of different faculty families for games in the evenings and these were unforgettable times as we sang, prayed, and laughed together. Our children, Jan Rune and Laila, had no access to the radio or television, we had no regular newspaper, and it was eight miles to the nearest phone. But they didn't feel isolated. They had a whole campus to explore, and friends living right next door.

As Jan Rune grew into a toddler, it became apparent he was an independent thinker—never content with simply being told; he had to find things out for himself. He was quick-minded, mischievous, and interested in everything.

One Sabbath, when Jan Rune was not yet two years of age, Jan had to preach at the campus church. It was at the end of the hot, dry season, and in the break between Sabbath School and the church service, Jan Rune announced he was thirsty—"Really thirsty, Mum!" Well, I had brought some purified water along, but Jan Rune and Laila had already drunk it all up during Sabbath School. I had no water to give Jan Rune, and I told him so.

"I want some more water," he insisted.

"Jan Rune, you'll have to just wait until Dad has finished preaching," I said. "Then we'll go straight home and I'll get you some more water."

We took our seats in the church and Jan rose to the pulpit to begin his sermon. Before I realized what was happening, Jan Rune was standing up on his chair and saying in a loud, clear voice, "Daddy! Daddy! Please say 'Amen.' "

The congregation exploded into laughter, and Jan felt compelled to preach a shorter sermon that day. That's our son, Jan Rune—a real "original."

An unusual pet

When we first arrived in Nigeria, we found we'd inherited a cat that had been owned by a family who'd gone back to the United States. She was beautiful, fluffy-white, and blue-eyed, and she immediately developed an extraordinary attachment to Jan. She must have sensed that he had a soft spot for animals. She would greet Jan when he walked through the door by rubbing up against his legs, and would love nothing more than to curl up on his lap while he stroked her back.

Unfortunately, she kept producing litters of kittens. On one memorable occasion, she delivered the first of her kittens just before Jan had to go down to the college to teach a class. Then, she seemed to wait. Within minutes of Jan returning home for lunch, she delivered two more of her kittens. Jan went back down for another class and she waited again. And then, on his return, she promptly delivered her final kitten.

In many ways these years were good. Most rewarding of all was seeing students growing, learning, and making a commitment to the Lord. So many of these young men and women went on to professional careers, and many have made huge contributions to the church in West Africa and internationally. Matthew Bediako, who served as general secretary of the Seventh-day Adventist world church, was one of many students from that time whom we remember fondly.

Yet, within a year or two of our arrival in Nigeria, the peaceful existence we'd taken for granted began to erode.

Biafran War

There are many different explanations for the cause of the Biafran War, the civil war which engulfed Nigeria in violence for almost three years. It began in July 1967, propelled by tribal rivalries, economic inequalities, and religious and ethnic tensions.

Its ultimate causes may be hard to pin down, but its consequences were unambiguous and cruel. As the Hausas of north Nigeria battled the Ibo (now often known as Igbo) of the southeast, an estimated one million men, women, and children died either from the fighting, or from the famine that followed in its wake.

The atmosphere on campus changed perceptibly, although we kept everything running as normally as possible. Some of the students had to leave, recalled by their families. Others were scared to leave the campus at all, fearful they'd be assaulted or worse. This was especially true for those who bore no distinctive tribal tattoo markings on their faces—there would be no questions asked if they encountered a soldier from a hostile tribe.

Most of the other foreign members of staff at the college were American citizens, and the Embassy at Lagos issued a command that Americans were to limit their travel. Jan, being Norwegian, was the only member of faculty who could venture off campus to do shopping for the school and run many other necessary errands. His work load increased exponentially. He was president, registrar, teacher, shopper, and driver, and he rarely had a full night's sleep.

In some ways, Jan and I were able to cope better than some of the other staff with the emotional toll the conflict took on everyone. We were children of Nazi-occupied Norway and we already knew, first-hand, the terrible consequences of war. We also knew how to "make do" when supplies in the local markets became less varied, and we couldn't buy the food we were used to. We simply substituted and used whatever was available.

In occupied Norway, though, we'd still experienced a certain type of normality, even with the presence of German soldiers in our towns. For the most part, people still got up and went about their daily business. But here in Nigeria's civil war, there was a nerve-shredding unpredictability about the violence around us.

Laila and Jan Rune saw things—terrible things—and I wish we could have shielded them more. Once, traveling to Lagos, we drove past a localized clash of some kind. There, in front of us, a man was being burnt alive, a gasoline-filled rubber tire alight around his shoulders.

Every time Jan walked out the door on his way to Lagos or Ibadan, I thought, *Will he come back?* Sometimes the fighting drew close to the college campus—at one point, just a few miles away. On nights like these, after the children were asleep in their beds, Jan and I would take our Scrabble board out of the cupboard and set it up on the bed between us and play until we felt tired enough to sleep. We had one Scrabble set in English and one in Norwegian. We always chose to play the Norwegian version. It was so much more difficult—and all the more effective for taking our minds off the war.

New challenges

In spite of the war, we still had to face other, more immediate challenges. One day when Jan Rune was three years old, he came down with a bout of diarrhea. Jan was away at the time in the West African country of Sierra Leone helping to run an evangelistic campaign. At first, I wasn't too concerned—diarrhea was something we all encountered at times. I simply gave Jan Rune plenty to drink and waited for the sickness to run its course. Except it didn't. Jan Rune's temperature kept rising, and he became more and more dehydrated.

A military curfew meant that I couldn't take Jan Rune to the Ile-Ife hospital, three hours' drive away. I knew from my training at the Berrien Springs County Hospital years ago that I needed to replace his electrolytes, so I gave him spoonful after spoonful of a mixture of water, sugar, and salt. The hours turned into days. I can't remember ever being so exhausted and I prayed for the strength to keep going, and for Jan Rune to somehow pull through. I kept spooning in the mixture, but Jan Rune's diarrhea began to mix with blood and I could see him weakening.

On the third day the military curfew was lifted and a neighbor drove us up to the hospital. The staff there confirmed that Jan Rune was suffering from both regular and amoebic dysentery. While they worked on him, someone led me to a bed and I slept for hours. When I awoke, it was to the news that Jan Rune was recovering well. It's hard to describe the relief and gratitude I felt.

When Jan came home from his evangelistic series soon afterward, he hardly recognized his little son. Just a few weeks earlier, Jan Rune had been a chubby, healthy little boy, and yet now he was very thin. But he had survived and we were profoundly grateful.

Against All Odds

Unwelcome guests

Tropical Africa constantly surprised us with its vast array of exotic parasites and bugs. One day, Laila was playing nearby when she stopped and said to me, "Look, Mom, I have a tunnel on my arm!"

I looked closely and was shocked to see something long and thin, at least two inches in length, moving under her skin. We couldn't take her to the hospital right way—another military curfew was in place—and so we were forced to wait and watch. One morning, Laila exclaimed, "Oh, look! He's turned around and he's crawling down now!" When we finally got her to Ile-Ife hospital, the doctor quickly diagnosed hook worm—the type typically carried by animals—and gave her medicine to kill the parasites.

Around the same time, I came down with a painful bout of filariasis, an illness caused by tiny threadlike round worms that enter your body through your skin and which can cause pain that mimics the intense ache of arthritis. Strangely enough, there are two types of filariasis—a night time and a day time version. In order to determine which type it is (and thus which medicine is needed), a doctor examines skin samples taken from the patient during the day and then again during the night.

Once again, I thanked God for medical science and for our access, however interrupted by the civil war, to the Ile-Ife hospital. And I also began to more fully understand how unpredictable— and short—life could be for the many men, women, and children around us who couldn't access medical care. It was a sobering lesson for me, but just one of many that would come my way in the years just ahead.

Chapter 12

"Turn Your Eyes Upon Jesus"

THERE'S A MENTAL IMAGE I have of my maternal grandmother. She lived with my grandfather on the side of a very steep, isolated mountain valley in Norway, a few hours west by bus from where my family lived. It was a long, narrow valley, but my grandparents lived on the sunny side, so every day their little house was bathed in both morning and afternoon sunshine.

In the late afternoon, as the sun started to get lower in the sky, my grandmother would go outside and walk to a small rocky ledge on the side of the mountain. In her clear, beautiful voice she'd call out a long, sing-song tune—not precisely a song, but very musical—which would echo down through the valley, signaling the cows to come home.

As the sound of her voice died away, you'd hear, far down below, the tinkle of the bell attached to the lead cow's neck as it led the herd up the steep, winding path toward home.

My childhood home was defined by the sound of my parents arguing. In contrast, my grandparents' house was a refuge of calm and I spent as much time there as I possibly could. That image of my grandmother calling home the cows came to symbolize for me all that was good and peaceful and safe.

Peace of mind is a tremendously valuable thing, but unfortunately rather difficult to cultivate, especially when our external situation, or our emotional state, is less than peaceful. Scripture provides plenty of examples of people who at times found peace of mind elusive. King Saul, tortured by his jealousy of David; Haman,

the prime minister of Persia, driven to self-destruction by his im-
placable hatred of the Jews; the "rich young ruler" caught between
spiritual duty and earthly desire; the apostle Peter enduring a "dark
night of the soul" after he denied the Lord; and, the list goes on.

Focusing on a beautiful or personally meaningful mental image
can be a powerful way to reach for inner peace, despite our circumstances. At various times throughout my life, it has sometimes
seemed that a particular image or memory—such as the vivid mental picture I have of my grandmother—has been a lifeline to me in
the midst of physical or emotional pain.

Interestingly, science bears this out. Many studies have shown
that focusing on something beautiful or peaceful can significantly
assist pain management in everything from osteoarthritis, to fibro-
myalgia, to post-operative recovery, and even in advanced stage
cancer.

Of course, as Christians, it's not a completely novel idea. In the
words of an old hymn we've so often sang:

Turn your eyes upon Jesus,
Look full in His wonderful face,
And the things of earth will grow strangely dim,
In the light of His glory and grace.

Guardian angels

The civil war in Nigeria intensified and the atmosphere on our
campus became increasingly defined by the uncertainty and violence that seemed to surround us.

Jan ran many risks during these years, but, as is his nature, he
took them in his stride. Whenever he ventured off campus on one
of his many errands, he had to pass through a number of military
checkpoints and Jan soon made friends with many of the soldiers.
He had a marvelous ability to joke with them, and he became very
"African" in his sense of humor.

Nevertheless, Jan had several near misses, including a time he
went into Ibadan with a college driver delivering a load of fresh

bread from the school bakery. It was excellent bread and in great demand in the surrounding towns. One of two regular drivers was a member of the Ibo tribe, from the east of Nigeria, and he was one of the very few Ibos who'd chosen to stay on at the college in spite of it being in territory held by tribal enemies.

He came to Jan one day and said, "I'm scared to go to Ibadan by myself. Won't you please come with me today?" So Jan did. They made their delivery without incident, but on the way home they were stopped at a temporary checkpoint that had just been set up along an open stretch of road. It was manned by soldiers of a rogue militia who spoke very little English and who had clearly been drinking palm wine. They pointed their machine guns at the Ibo driver and ordered him out of the car—it seemed they meant to "deal" with him in the same brutal way that so many young men had been dealt with in this war; casually slain because of tribal identity.

Jan told the young man to stay where he was, uttered an urgent prayer, and then began talking to the soldiers. To this day, Jan doesn't know what he said, but he knows he spoke in English without pause for fifteen minutes or so. Finally, one of the soldiers spoke in halting English to the Ibo driver. "All right, we'll let you continue on, but only because your master talked so well."

Jan and I have often pondered this escape and have come to the conclusion that, however you want to explain it, it was the Holy Spirit's work.

On another occasion, a new missionary family from America arrived on campus, and among the shipment of goods they brought with them was a drum of household items for another missionary family living in Lagos. Somehow, we had to get this drum to the capital city, along a route marked by military checkpoints.

So, Jan strapped the drum to the roof of the college van for the one-hour journey south. Unfortunately, the drum was locked and Jan didn't have the key—it was with the family in Lagos. If Jan was stopped at a military checkpoint, he'd have no way of opening the drum for inspection and it was very unlikely that he'd be allowed to proceed.

Against All Odds

As he neared the first checkpoint, Jan looked in his rearview mirror and caught sight of a motorcade, obviously escorting a high official of some kind along the road toward Lagos. Jan pulled over to let it pass, then pulled in behind, sailing through the checkpoint in the wake of the motorcade. As he checked his rearview mirror again, he saw a group of soldiers standing, staring after this van with a metal drum lashed to its roof. All the way into Lagos, Jan tailed his "protector" and made it through every checkpoint with no questions asked.

Sometime later a letter arrived at the college telling us a carload of missionaries, fleeing violence in the north of the country, was coming to stay and would need to be housed and fed for some time. We didn't have enough food to care for these extras, so Jan withdrew £25 from the business office, and headed into Ibadan to buy supplies.

As he left the local village and turned onto the main road, he came across a strange tableau. There were two bicycles lying on the road, a car off to one side, two men in flowing robes, and two other men standing on the edge of the road holding their heads. Jan's immediate thought was that the car had hit the bicycles, so he pulled over to help.

It was a mistake. Within seconds of him stopping, a gun appeared through the open window of his car. Jan had earlier stuck his billfold with the £25 down by the side of his seat. The men in robes, pointing their guns at Jan, motioned for him to get out of the car and turn out his pockets. They were empty. Growing increasingly agitated, one of the men thrust the muzzle of his gun hard into the back of Jan's white shirt, making it clear that if Jan didn't produce something of value, there would be dire consequences. Jan pointed to where his billfold was hidden and they were satisfied.

The men who Jan had first seen were meat sellers on their way home from the market, carrying that day's profits. They'd been forced off the road, robbed, and then pistol-whipped by the thieves.

Jan was angry. The thieves had taken his car keys, but the car we had at the time—a German-made Opel—had a mechanism by which he could restart the motor without a key, providing the ignition had not been turned completely off. So Jan drove on, chasing after the attackers, and soon he had them within his sight. Jan thought if the car ahead of them was forced to stop at a military checkpoint, perhaps he could convince the soldiers to take the thieves into custody.

But as the car he was pursuing disappeared around a blind corner, Jan suddenly had second thoughts about the wisdom of his plan. He stopped, turned around, and headed back toward the college.

I was at a neighbor's house in their living room, while the children were out on the porch doing schoolwork, and that's where Jan found me.

"Jan, you can't be back from Ibadan already," I said.

Jan, with his usual cheerful voice, said, "Sorry, dear. I was held up, so I had to come back."

"Jan, you shouldn't joke about things like that," I said.

"Would you have a glass of water?" Jan asked our neighbor. "I need a drink."

"There's water in the kitchen," she said. "Help yourself."

We watched as Jan turned to head into the kitchen. And on the back of his shirt we clearly saw the mark where the muzzle of the gun had been pressed into his back."

"Jan, you really *did* have a hold-up, didn't you?" I said.

"Well, Kari, my dear, I just told you I did," he replied.

Health scares

Throughout our years in Nigeria, I kept getting reoccurring infections—sometimes respiratory-type infections, sometimes a urinary tract infection. For some reason, I was taking longer and longer to recover from these bouts of sickness, anywhere between six weeks and a couple of months. And these infections were becoming more and more debilitating. On more than one occasion, Jan had to take me to the hospital to recover, or to be rehydrated with an IV drip. But during the in-between times, I was fine. We were young. We had a sense of purpose, and a strong feeling that we were where the Lord wanted us to be. So we dismissed these bouts of sickness with the explanation to ourselves, and others, that "Africa just doesn't seem to agree with Kari!"

Around this time, Jan had a health scare of his own. We had a couple of visitors at the college who needed to get to Ethiopia, but heavy fighting had closed the airport in Lagos. The only way for them to get out of the country was to drive a day's journey across the Nigerian border, through what is now Benin and Togo and into Ghana.

"Kari, I've got to take them to Accra, but I don't want to leave you and the children here," said Jan.

So Laila, Jan Rune, and I piled into the car with Jan and the two visitors, and we began the long journey. Our route through Togo and Benin ran parallel to the Atlantic Ocean coastline for many, many miles and the white sand and the tropical sun produced a terrible glare. Unfortunately, Jan had forgotten to bring his sunglasses, but he drove on through the piercing white light. We reached Accra and delivered our guests to the airport. We spent the night there, and when we woke up in the morning, Jan said, "It's a strange thing, Kari, but you don't look like you have any arms."

He could see part of me, but not the whole. It was his left eye that was the problem; he had lost a whole swathe of his vision. The treasurer of our college had been in Accra, and he offered to drive us back to Nigeria. Over the next few days, the sight in Jan's left eye continued to deteriorate, so we drove into Lagos so he could get specialized attention. The medical consensus was that Jan needed to go back to Europe for treatment, so he left for Norway and I waited anxiously with the children.

The following Saturday evening there was a social get-together at the college, and a couple of workers from the nearby hospital were visiting the campus and came along too. During the evening, the conversation turned to Jan's eyesight problem and the symptoms he'd been experiencing.

"Well, it sounds like a brain tumor," these medical workers said confidently. "That's probably what it is."

I was aghast. A tumor? I hadn't even considered the possibility. And the level of my anxiety shot up. Meanwhile, back in Oslo, Jan was enduring a round of medical tests. Finally, the doctors agreed the problem was a swelling of the fluids behind the eye caused by the intense glare from the sun on the white sand during his drive to Accra without sunglasses. Ironically, this condition is also sometimes found in Scandinavia, where the strong reflection of the sun off snow and ice can cause trauma to the eyes. The only remedy was rest and dark glasses, so Jan flew up to his mother's home in north Norway and slept and slept and slept, and slowly his vision returned.

Newbold College

Jan had decided that he wanted to get his doctorate in theology, and so he began applying to different universities. He was accepted into a university in Scotland and Germany. He eventually settled on the Universität Tübingen, one of Europe's oldest universities, located in a beautiful, medieval city in southwestern Germany.

Six weeks before we were due to leave Nigeria for Germany, however, we had a call from the church division office in St. Albans, England. Would we be willing to first spend a couple of years at Newbold College in England, where they needed a new head for their theology department? After two years teaching at Newbold, we were told, Jan could have study leave to pursue his doctorate in Germany.

We prayed about it, but didn't feel strongly attracted to the idea. Yet, we decided to accept. It was an official call from the church, and so possibly this was where God wanted us to be.

As we were preparing to leave, word came that expatriate women and children from our area might need to be evacuated. Since our whole family was due to leave soon, Jan and I decided that the children and I would travel to England ahead of him, sailing the next day from Lagos. Jan would follow later by plane.

For me, the boat journey was a slow reacclimation to the norms and customs of the West. For Laila and Jan Rune, the change was more dramatic—they were leaving all they had ever known and were being thrust into an environment that seemed quite foreign to them.

The first night on board the ship, all the passengers were invited to attend a special drinks reception in one of the salons. It sounded somewhat formal to me, so I carefully dressed the children in their Sabbath-best clothes, which I'd made from red and black African-print material from the local market near the college. It took me longer to decide what to wear. After years of wearing light, breezy clothes suited to the African climate, I decided that for this special occasion I should probably wear stockings with my Sabbath dress. Little Jan Rune was fascinated by this strange new item of clothing I was wearing.

Both children were very excited—I'd promised they'd be able to get a glass of apple juice at the reception, and they were anxious to have their first taste of this exotic drink.

We found the salon and joined the other passengers, Laila on my right and Jan Rune on my left, with me in the middle feeling somewhat shy. Jan Rune, never one to stand back, decided to break the ice. "Look what my mum's got on!" he said in a loud voice to everyone gathered around. And in a flash, he'd lifted the skirt of my dress up high so that everyone had a good view. "She's wearing stockings!"

If I hadn't known it before, I was reminded that our children had a lot of adjusting ahead of them. And not just them, but Jan and me, as well. We were headed for a new country, a new culture, a new "mission field."

A new world

Leaving Africa was a tremendous upheaval for our children. Apart from furlough back to Norway, this had been their entire world. They had become as African as two Norwegian children could be. At night when he said his prayers, Jan Rune would sometimes ask God to change his blond hair and white skin to something a little more "normal." For them, the Newbold College campus in Binfield, South England, surrounded by wooded hills and meadows, was a strange and foreign place, filled with odd people who had even odder customs.

Often in Nigeria, as our family car had rattled along the dusty roads, it would attract the attention of a group of children by the side of the road. They'd wave and chase after the car, calling, "White man! White man!" in the local Yoruba language.

One day shortly after we'd arrived at Newbold, our family was standing in front of the college administration building, alongside which ran a busy street. Jan Rune, then just five years old, began to wave at cars as they passed by and shouting out after them in Yoruba, "White man! White man!"

After a few minutes, he turned away, looking somewhat discouraged. "There are too many of those white people here," he said to me. "I just can't keep waving at all those cars!"

That night during family worship, Jan Rune did not ask God to give him the black hair and skin he'd wanted for so long.

Chapter 13
Limitations

A MERICAN THEOLOGIAN REINHOLD NIEBUHR IS credited with writing the now famous "Serenity Prayer." It first appeared in one of his 1943 sermons, and later as a contribution to a prayer book for military chaplains.

"God, grant me the serenity to accept the things I cannot change,
The courage to change the things I can,
And wisdom to know the difference."

This prayer has become somewhat of a cliché; in the decades since it has been reprinted on everything from coffee mugs to key chains. But its sheer ubiquity shouldn't overshadow the profound truth it communicates.

How does one identify that fine line between our legitimate and imagined limitations? How does one tread the path between an attitude of wise acceptance, and simply giving up?

From the time since I'd recovered from my heart surgery as a young girl until I contracted cerebral malaria at thirty years of age, I'd come to think of myself as invulnerable. Young people often do. I was energetic, full of plans, and ready for whatever life would bring.

In the years following our time in Africa, I had to embark on a crash course on learning to live with limitations, and it's been a continuing education ever since.

Two key ideas I've learned are "reframing success" and "being kind to myself."

Limitations

Sometimes circumstances demand that we abandon our perfect ideal—whether it's related to our career, our physical abilities, or even our relationships. It's not easy, but it's easier than living with the constant ache of unattainable expectations.

Instead, we have to find other ways to define what success means to us, within our unique set of circumstances.

And all along the way, we need to speak kindly to ourselves. I've learned to say at times, "Well done, Kari. You did it!" even if my achievement, objectively viewed, is rather insignificant. But if it's something that required discipline of mind or body, or the overcoming of some obstacle, then acknowledging that is a good thing. When we speak with family, colleagues, or friends, it doesn't take long to realize that a critical, fault-finding tone doesn't bring out the best in anyone. So why do we so often speak unkindly to ourselves? Why dwell unnecessarily on the negative?

There's a chapter in Ellen White's book *The Ministry of Healing* that has shaped my thinking on this point to no small degree. In the chapter entitled "Mind Cure," she writes, "Nothing tends more to promote health of body and of soul than does a spirit of gratitude and praise. It is a positive duty to resist melancholy, discontented thoughts and feelings—as much a duty as it is to pray. If we are heaven-bound, how can we go as a band of mourners, groaning and complaining all along the way to our Father's house?"*

I've taken to heart Mrs. White's suggestion that no matter what limitations we struggle with, "there is hope for you in Christ. God does not bid us overcome in our own strength. He asks us to come close to His side. Whatever difficulties we labor under, which weigh down soul and body, He waits to make us free."**

First symptoms

I have a photo from our first winter in England, where I'm standing with a group of people smiling into the lens of the camera. What stands out—glaringly, in hindsight—is the difference between

---

* *The Ministry of Healing* (2003), 251.
** Ibid., 249.

my face and those of the others in the group. In contrast to everyone else's pasty-white winter skin, my face is glowing with a vibrant bronze tan.

Of course, to an endocrinologist my various symptoms were all pieces of a puzzle that fit together to form the perfect image of someone with Addison's disease; someone whose adrenal cortex, the small glands located above each kidney which produce steroids for the body, were in sharp decline. My very tan skin; the brown spots in my mouth; my periodic craving for salt; the growing frequency and severity of different infections I picked up; the difficulty I had in "bouncing back" afterward.

Jan and I, however, had no way of seeing the complete picture. We were dealing in fragments, and treated each illness as it came along as a separate, unrelated occurrence. It was annoying and often difficult to deal with, but it was just part of our lives.

However, as our family adjusted from the African tropics to the bitter cold of our first British winter, I began to pick up colds and other infections with greater frequency, and we began to suspect that perhaps something more serious was going on. Still, we had no way of knowing what this thing could be.

Reshaping my dreams

It didn't take long for us to form what would be a lifelong affection for Newbold College. This liberal arts college in southeast England was established in 1901 and has trained generations of Adventist young people from Britain, other countries across the church's Trans-European division, and the rest of the world.

During those first two years at Newbold, Jan was kept very busy. He was head of the theology department and taught full time, but he arranged his classes in such a way that he had two days most weeks to go down to London to continue research for his doctoral studies.

During the first summer vacation, the college sponsored Jan to travel to Tübingen where he undertook intensive classes in Latin and German in preparation for his upcoming full-time studies. But the summer of 1969 was memorable for another reason as well. On July 20, astronaut Neil Armstrong walked on the moon and somehow the words of the song "Lift up the trumpet and loud let it ring; Jesus is coming again!" became more real to me than ever before. The blurry news images of humans walking on the moon seemed to give extra power to the picture, long-held in my imagination, of Jesus returning in the clouds of heaven.

Our two years at Newbold flew past and as we got ready to move to Germany for Jan's doctoral studies, I became pregnant again with Rein Andre, our third child. Through all our years in the United States, Africa, and Britain, I'd held on to a certainty that somehow, sometime, I'd return to my studies. It was more than just a hope for me; I was convinced that this is what I would do and I was certain it was the path God intended for my life.

But with two young children, another on the way, and a mysterious illness that had Jan and I increasingly worried, my certainty began to waver. Slowly, I was relinquishing my dream for further study, and it was a painful process.

Children have a wonderful way of cutting to the heart of an issue. A decade or so after this difficult time, Rein Andre came home from school one day to find me lying on the sofa battling one of my Addison's episodes. He's always had a very analytical, logical mind.

He looked at me thoughtfully for a while, then said, "Mum, aren't you glad you got me instead of that stupid doctorate you always wanted. Look at you now—a doctorate would have been useless to you!"

How right he was! The birth of our much-loved third child completed our family.

My pregnancy with Rein, however, was very difficult. We were in the midst of packing up and preparing to move the family to Germany and much of the work fell on Jan's shoulders.

When we arrived in Tübingen we enrolled the children into school, Jan settled into his studies at the university, and I began a routine of checking in at the hospital every Monday morning for tests and monitoring. I would go each time with a packed suitcase, just in case I had to be admitted.

Against All Odds

At the six-month mark of my pregnancy, I began to hemorrhage after my doctor performed an amniocentesis test on me, and so I was admitted to the hospital for observation and bed rest. During my stay, I found my language skills stretched to the limit as I tried to communicate with the nurses and other hospital staff. I'd learned German at school, but in the intervening years all my German-language ability seemed to have deserted me. But necessity is a wonderful teacher, and I soon discovered how quickly you can learn vital German words such as *"Bettpfanne"* (bedpan) when the need is there!

Completing the family

At the seven-month mark of my pregnancy, my bilirubin level rose too high and the doctor induced labor. A nurse inserted the IV line and started the drip, and Jan left the hospital to attend a lecture and then get the children home from school.

I've always had quick deliveries and this was no exception. Before long, Rein had been born and I craned my neck to catch a glimpse of my baby before the doctor whisked him away. I saw that we'd had a boy, but he looked black and completely lifeless. A knot of nurses surrounded the doctor as they rushed Rein from the room and I was left, not knowing if my child would survive.

No one came back to me that afternoon to tell me anything about my baby. The nurses I asked fobbed off my questions. I had no way of contacting Jan—we had no phone.

For the first time in my life, I got a migraine. The headache grew so bad that I began to vomit and when Jan finally came in the evening, he found me in a terrible state. There were three other new mothers in the room with me, and each of them had seen and nursed her baby. I was distraught.

Our baby wasn't in the nursery with the other newborns—he was still being treated—but late that evening, Jan was finally able to talk with the doctor. They'd changed Rein's blood, but the bilirubin had again risen too high and the doctor was concerned. Rein's reflexes, however, looked fine.

Limitations

I insisted on seeing our baby, so the nurses put me in a wheel-chair and Jan wheeled me down the hall to the big window that opened into the nursery. At the very back of the room in the infant ICU section, a nurse held up a little bundle who had a profusion of lines and tubes emerging from him. The next day I went home, but Rein stayed.

After a couple of weeks, the pediatrician caring for Rein told us we could take our baby home if we had a nurse for him. But how could we, on our half-salary, afford a nurse?

We'd been attending the local Seventh-day Adventist Church in Tübingen, and after initial wariness on the part of some church members ("An Adventist pastor studying theology at a Lutheran university! Can that be right?"), our family had been warmly embraced. There was a retired pediatric nurse who also attended the church, and she heard of our dilemma and offered her services. Within days, Marta had become one of our family. She took to Rein immediately and to the other two children as well, and in the short time she was with us, she became a beloved "grandmother" to us all.

Rein Andre had severe anemia and I was determined I was going to get his iron levels up. I studied everything I could find on nutrition and began blending spinach, beets, and apricots. Before Rein was a year old, his iron had reached normal levels and his pediatrician couldn't believe it had been done on a vegetarian diet. "But Mrs. Paulsen, how much liver did you *really* feed him?" he asked.

When Rein was three months old, the division asked Jan to return temporarily to the college in Nigeria as a caretaker principal for a few months. The children and I stayed in Germany and it was a difficult time. We didn't have much money and couldn't afford a proper change table for Rein. I seemed to spend a lot of time bending over to change him on the floor, or to bathe him in a little plastic tub I'd put down in the bath. Perhaps it was all the bending combined with the chill of winter, but one morning I woke up and I literally couldn't move. My back was in agony.

Laila was ten years old and extremely capable for her age. Over the next few days, I gave her and Jan Rune directions from my bed, but it was their intelligence and common sense that allowed them to care for their baby brother, do the shopping and cooking, and keep the household running.

Tübingen, Germany

In between family dramas in Tübingen, Jan had settled into a disciplined study regime. He would get up very early and work for several hours, take a short break, and then work for another few hours. He'd then wheel Rein Andre out in his pram for an outing to a nearby park or along a walking trail. I can still see Jan in my memory, sitting in our living room typing on his old typewriter, utterly absorbed in his work.

We'd been extremely fortunate in our accommodations in Tübingen. On one of his earlier summer visits to the university, Jan was introduced to someone who, through a chain of mutual acquaintances, had heard of a couple who were planning a year-long trip to Australia to visit their married daughter. This couple offered Jan their lovely townhouse in an affluent part of the city for very low rent. Most of the other married students had accommodations out in the surrounding villages, but we counted ourselves lucky to be so close to the university.

We met many interesting people from so many different walks of life and religious traditions—theologians, fellow students, medical doctors. We became close friends with many of them and, as they got to know us, we hoped we were helping break down prejudices about people of "nontraditional" faiths.

Directly across the road from our townhouse was a Roman Catholic family, whose children often played with ours. Laila and Jan Rune would be in and out of their house, or invite them over to ours. For one reason or another, though, I'd never had the chance to properly get to know the children's mother.

One day I was walking to the local store, pushing Rein Andre in his pram. My neighbor was coming the other way, holding her youngest child by the hand.

She introduced herself in German, and said, "Mrs. Paulsen, I've wanted to talk to you for a long time. I have a question for you."

"Yes, of course, what is it?" I replied.

"Your children always leave our house late Friday afternoon and don't come back until Sunday. I asked Jan Rune why, and he said, 'That's when Sabbath starts.' So I asked him, 'What do you do on Sabbath?' And he said, 'We eat fruit and pray.' "

"Mrs. Paulsen," she added. "I can't even take my children to mass, they won't sit quietly, and yet it seems that yours pray all day!"

I laughed. "Well, it's not as holy as it sounds." I explained that on our limited budget we allowed the children two pieces of fruit each week day, but as a special Sabbath treat they could eat all the fruit they wanted on Friday evening. And as for the praying? There *was* extra worship time on Sabbath, but it was far from being a twenty-four-hour prayer vigil, I assured her.

"Oh, thank God," she said. "You're normal." And from that time on our friendship grew. During our second year in Tübingen, they went to the United States for a year. They knew that the owners of the townhouse we were currently living in would soon return from Australia, so they offered us their apartment, at an even lower rent than we had been paying.

Linguists of necessity

Laila and Jan Rune were becoming adept at adjusting to different cultures. We'd enrolled them in the local school at Tübingen, where the staff told us Jan Rune and Laila would need a German-language tutor if we wanted them to keep up with their school work. Hiring a tutor was far beyond our limited finances, so when the children came home from school each day, Jan would help Laila with her homework, and I would help Jan Rune.

That system worked well for the first three months, but then Rein Andre was born in November, and everything changed. Jan and I no longer had time to devote to translating German home-work for the children. So instead, we gave them a German-English dictionary and told them they'd have to do it on their own. And they did! In Germany, children of Laila's age had to sit an exam which would determine whether they would be streamed into a more academic school the following year, or if they'd go, instead, to a more practical, vocation-oriented school. Laila was a foreigner, new to the German language, and yet she passed the exam and qualified for the academic stream. We were so proud of her determination in the face of the challenges she'd had to overcome.

Herr Doktor Paulsen

At the end of our two years, Jan was called to defend his thesis before a panel of venerable examiners during an oral exam called a *Rigorosum,* which was dreaded by every doctoral candidate. The day before he was due to undergo this ordeal, Jan ran into a fellow doctoral student who had defended *his* thesis the day before. The report Jan heard was not reassuring. This friend of Jan's—one of the brightest in the university—had failed.

The next day, Jan was incredibly nervous. He answered the many questions posed to him in German. And then he left the room to sit outside while his fate was considered.

The door opened and someone motioned Jan back inside. The senior examiner spoke. "Congratulations, *Herr Doktor* Paulsen!" he said, and smiled.

It was time to return to Newbold College.

Chapter 14

Laugh or Cry—a Choice

A UNIVERSAL THEME THAT LINKS TOGETHER so many varieties of human suffering is this: You can't schedule a crisis. It'll come to you, whether it happens to be convenient or not. When life's cataclysms strike—whether it's the death of someone we love, a frightening medical report, the breakup of a family, losing a job, or many other possible stresses, large and small—they all come on their own timetable and we have no choice but to cope.

Renowned Austrian psychologist Viktor Frankl spent more than three years in Nazi-controlled ghettos and work camps, and one year at the notorious Auschwitz concentration camp. He was stripped of his freedom, his possessions, and his dignity. One of the most dehumanizing aspects of his imprisonment was the loss of his name. He became instead a number, "119104," which was sewn onto the front of his shirt. Then, when he was finally liberated in 1945, he learned his pregnant wife had died in the Bergen-Belsen concentration camp, his mother had been gassed at Auschwitz, and his brother had died as he'd labored in a work gang attached to the Auschwitz camp.

One of the many books Frankl wrote in the years that followed this experience is simply titled, *Nevertheless, Say "Yes" to Life.* This was a theme woven throughout his groundbreaking development of so-called "Logotherapy"—a school of psychological theory based on the premise that humans can't avoid suffering, but we do have some level of control over our response. If we can somehow find the meaning, the "logos," in our suffering—if we can identify and hold on to some transcendent values—then we'll not only survive, but find a sense of contentment, even happiness.

Frankl's 1997 obituary in the *New York Times* quoted one his most famous observations that "the last of the human freedoms" is to "choose one's attitude in any given set of circumstances."*

It sounds like a lofty, impossible-to-reach ideal. Maybe even a "Pollyanna-ish" denial of how devastating life's blows can be.

Yet, given Frankl's own credentials in the realm of suffering, it gives one pause for thought.

It's a philosophy, also, that fits well with what we know of the "great controversy" between good and evil, which is the genesis of human pain. We may have no choice but to endure in the here and now, but as followers of Christ, we have our eyes fixed ahead, to the grand finale that's coming.

I think of the early Christian believers, who endured exile or persecution for the sake of their new, "subversive" beliefs. Acts 5 recounts the arrest of some of the apostles for preaching and healing in Jerusalem. They were imprisoned, brought up before the Sanhedrin, harangued and jeered, and finally flogged for good measure. Yet verse 41 of that chapter records that "the apostles left the Sanhedrin, rejoicing because they had been counted worthy of suffering disgrace for the Name (NIV)".

I don't think they "rejoiced" because their physical discomfort was somehow less than real. But their long-view perspective—their knowledge of God's big-picture plan—was more compelling than what was happening in the short-term.

I believe, as Frankl suggests, that our basic attitude toward life dictates a great deal about how we respond to difficulties. Managing our attitude, though, is often no easy task.

My husband, Jan, has always had an extraordinary ability to laugh and to find the humor in situations, even when things seem particularly grim. Sometimes during my illness, I'd say to him, "I really don't see how you can smile now, Jan."

---

* Holcomb B. Noble, "Dr. Viktor E. Frankl of Vienna, Psychiatrist of the Search for Meaning, Dies at 92" *New York Times,* September 4, 1997.

Laugh or Cry—a Choice

And he'd reply, "Well, you have a choice, don't you? You can either cry or smile, and I'd much prefer to smile."

A turn for the worse

The house we moved into when we returned to Newbold College from Tübingen was a one-hundred-year-old gatekeeper's cottage—it was cold and primitive. It wasn't so bad when we arrived in August, but by the time Rein Andre turned two years old in November of that year, we were shivering.

Addison's disease had really only been "toying" with me up until this point. I still didn't have a name for my frequent bouts of illness, but even though I sometimes had to go to the hospital, I always eventually recovered and returned to a semblance of my old self.

However, in the following spring of 1973, the course of my Addison's took a decisive and permanent turn for the worse.

Jan had gone to Denmark to conduct a week of prayer at Vejlefjordskolen, our old junior college at Daugård. While he was away, I came down with one of my perennial UTIs. But this time I was very ill, indeed. I couldn't keep food down and my blood pressure dropped to a new low. I was admitted to the hospital for a time, but the doctors there really didn't know what they were treating. I came home, and continued to go to the hospital every week for monitoring. I vomited and vomited every day. I had a terrible craving for salt and my weight plummeted to just 48 kilograms (105 pounds).

We'd planned to go to Norway in the summer for a teacher's convention. I felt I could manage the trip if I took things very easy. Unfortunately, the crossing from England to Norway was very rough, and my seasickness set off another bout of vomiting. As soon as we got off the boat, Jan drove me to an Adventist doctor we knew in Oslo.

This doctor wasn't an endocrinologist, he was a general internist, but he asked Jan many, many questions about my medical history. He noted my unusually tanned skin and looked at the brown spots in my mouth.

"Jan, I think she has an illness called Addison's," he said. It was the first time we'd heard of such a disease. He took a blood test and sent it off for analysis, but started me immediately on a course of cortisone acetate. It was a type of cortisone that we later discovered my body couldn't properly metabolize, but it was enough to turn the tide on the Addison's crisis into which I'd gradually been sinking.

From that moment on, I made it my mission to educate myself as far as I could about the disease that had disrupted our lives so much. I was amazed by how little medical literature was available— although that shouldn't have been so surprising considering how few people actually suffer from the disease. Addison's is neither widely known, nor widely studied, and perhaps for this reason, new treatments have been slow in coming. From reading and talking with endocrinologists, I realized that since first contracting cerebral malaria in Ghana, I'd been dealing with episodes of acute Addison's—periods of time where the level of cortisone production by my body had dropped dangerously low. But then somehow, each time, my damaged adrenal cortex had righted itself enough to keep on going.

Then, in 1973, my Addison's had become chronic. My adrenal cortex was effectively "dead." My production of cortisone had dwindled to almost nothing, and without steroid supplementation, I could not have survived long.

It's chronic

I finally had a diagnosis, and the steroid medication I was taking, if not entirely effective, was at least keeping me alive. I suppose I'd always clung to the idea that my illness was a difficult but temporary intrusion into our lives. But now, I began slowly to come to terms with the reality of living with a chronic illness and it was not an easy mental transition to make.

Time and again, Jan's "default setting" of calm good humor in the face of hardship got us through many of the bumps of everyday life. Around this time, a doctor made a mistake in my Addison's medication, which caused problems with my heart. I was sent to visit a cardiologist in London, who prescribed a short-term course of heart medication to take until things settled down.

Jan and I left the cardiologist's office and walked toward where our car was parked, and all the while I kept up a running commentary. I was upset, and for once I gave full vent to my feelings. It was utterly unfair, I declared, that someone else's mistake had caused this problem. "And now I have to go on this awful medication and worry about my heart, on top of everything else!"

Without much hesitation came Jan's reply. "Kari, I don't think we need to worry about your heart. It will last just as long as the rest of you."

I had to sit down on some nearby steps—I couldn't stop laughing. His comment was true, timely, and just what I needed. So often through the years, Jan's astute and humorous observations have saved me from a lot of worries.

At times, it was awkward explaining my Addison's disease to others, especially since I had no obvious "wound" or disability. One Sabbath when Jan was away, I awoke drained of energy yet determined to go to church. The effort to get dressed and walk from our house to the college church was almost more than I could manage, but I made it and I sat down in the pew both exhausted and pleased with what I'd accomplished. Prayer was announced and as the congregation knelt, I stayed in my seat and prayed, *Lord, if I kneel down I don't think I'll get back up.*

As the prayer ended and people again took their seats, a man leaned toward me and whispered, "Sister Paulsen, you ought to be ashamed of yourself."

I've never forgotten the hurtfulness of that moment. Why do we so often feel compelled to judge the motives, or even the spirituality, of others? I believe there are few things more destructive within the body of Christ than a superior attitude that seeks out faults in others. Perhaps we'd do well to keep in mind the well-known saying, "Every saint has a past and every sinner has a future." For in the final analysis, we're all in this together—each one of us has as much need of God's grace and forgiveness as the next person.

A wider mission field

The next few years flew by for us. In 1976, Jan was asked to be president at Newbold College, and then at the 1980 General Conference Session in Dallas, Texas, he was elected general secretary and education director for the Adventist Church in the Northern European Division(now known as the Trans-European Division)—an administrative district headquartered in St. Albans, England.

Then, just three years later, the division president, Pastor Walter Scragg, was called to a new position in the United States, and Jan was elected to fill his place.

In terms of distance, our move from Newbold College to St. Albans was only about forty-five miles—the shortest move we'd ever made. We didn't even have a new language to master or new customs to learn!

But, in reality, it was a big and somewhat difficult transition for our family, especially for our children who loved Newbold and the many friends they had there. I also missed the campus where I felt part of a bustling community.

St. Albans is a beautiful cathedral town, with a high street lined with centuries-old shops and buildings. It's a lovely place to live. But the key difference for me was that the homes of the division staff were scattered around the city. There was no easy way to socialize or keep up-to-date with everyone's news and it was a big difference to the Newbold life. Jan and I had always worked as partners, but now he was traveling a lot or at the office. What could I do that would be of value to others?

It was around this time that I developed a habit that has stayed with me ever since. I began to keep my ears open for information about people who were sick, or who were going through a difficult time, and I made it my mission to phone them regularly. I soon added the names of some former students who I knew were no longer attending church. The number of people on my "phone ministry" list grew and once again I began to feel a sense of mission—a sense that I was involved in God's work in some way, no matter how small my contribution.

Laugh or Cry—a Choice

During the twelve years Jan was president of the Trans-European Division, I grew to love England more and more. In all, we lived in England for twenty-five years—the longest we've spent in any one country—and the friends we made during this time continue to be a blessing to us.

Through this period, Jan and I carried on our private tradition of discussing this, that, and everything else in between. This is how our relationship began when we first met back at the junior college in Denmark, and today it's still the way we process every issue or challenge that comes our way. In many ways, our partnership has been based on a mutual love of conversation. There are some topics we've kept strictly off limits—confidential personnel matters from work, for instance, or committee discussions that have been deemed confidential. But apart from this, Jan's willingness to share and to discuss issues back and forth has allowed me to feel that I'm truly a partner in his work.

Elusive answers

While we served in England, I continued to search for a better way to stabilize my Addison's. I was still taking cortisone acetate daily, but I had no way of knowing at the time that my body wasn't capable of metabolizing this form of cortisone properly. Every endocrinologist I consulted was puzzled that I failed to respond to the regular steroid doses. Their answer was always to keep increasing the strength of my medication, and so my daily steroid dose went up and up and up. Anyone who's taken steroids for any length of time can tell you that, in the short term, an increased dose definitely helps. But over time, the effectiveness of the medication plateaus and you're back at square one.

Twice, Jan and I got together the money for me to travel to Loma Linda University Medical Center in California to see a specialist endocrinologist. I did these trips on a shoestring budget, staying at a hospital guesthouse, and even asking the medical staff to leave a cannula in my arm so that I could do some of the many required blood draws by myself. Still, no matter how many doctors I consulted or how many tests they ran, a solution to controlling my Addison's remained elusive.

In 1984, some friends from the United States, Derek and Bodil, were visiting England and came to our house for a meal. We'd known Bodil for many years. As an eighteen-year-old, she'd traveled from America to attend Newbold College and she'd been one of our youngest students. Her father, who we'd known from our days in the States, was an administrator at the National Institutes of Health in Washington, D.C.—a world-renowned medical research facility, usually called by its acronym, the NIH.

"Kari, what you're going through just doesn't make sense," said Bodil, who was a nurse. "You really need to get to the bottom of it. You should go to the NIH."

"How on earth could I do that?" I asked.

"Well, you go to your primary care doctor and he sends your papers to the NIH," she said. "They'll let you know if there's a study they're running that matches your particular condition. And if you're accepted, all your medical treatment will be free."

She added, "Kari, the medical care you'd receive there would be second-to-none."

That week, I asked my doctor to send off my paperwork to the NIH, although I held out little hope there'd be a suitable study underway.

Within three weeks, the NIH responded saying they'd found me a place in a newly started program—or "protocol"—which had recently been set up to study endocrine disorders such as mine. My timing—or more precisely, the Lord's timing—was impeccable.

Return to D.C.

Within a week, I was on my way to Washington, D.C., and during the long flight I ran through a whole gamut of emotions—fear, skepticism, hope. I arrived at Dulles Airport and Bodil's parents picked me up and later took me to the NIH facility in Bethesda, Maryland, where my particular protocol would be conducted.

Jan and I had agreed that my stay at the NIH should be for five weeks. Laila was studying in the United States and Jan Rune in

London, so there was now just eleven-year-old Rein Andre at home. Our plan was for Jan to care for Rein while I was away, and I'd fly back to England in time for Jan to fly to the United States to attend a church leadership meeting known as Annual Council.

I was checked in at the NIH and underwent a series of tests. After a time, I met with one of the study's endocrinologists.

"Mrs. Paulsen, you're currently taking eighty milligrams of cortisone a day," he said. "But for a woman of your height and weight the correct dosage is twenty-five milligrams. Before we can do anything else, we need to get you off this high dose, and back down to the appropriate level."

It sounded reasonable to me, but then he added the "kicker."

"I need to be honest with you," he said. "Withdrawal from steroids—especially from the high-level dose you're on—is not going to be easy." What a tremendous understatement.

The first withdrawal symptom I noticed was a headache that grew and grew in intensity until I was crying out with the pain. The hospital staff wouldn't give me any pain medication—it wasn't allowed in case it threw off the results of their study. (They were carefully measuring everything—how much water and food they gave me, what my symptoms were; they watched and noted everything.)

The best remedy they could offer was to pack my head in ice in an attempt to ease the pain. There was no mercy and the near-constant round of tests continued.

My five weeks was up and so, against the advice of the NIH doctors, I insisted on being discharged. I was driven to Dulles Airport in an ambulance and wheeled on board the plane. One of my doctors had spoken with the airline and arranged for me to have four empty seats so I could stretch out in relative comfort.

As the plane taxied and took off, I become uncomfortably aware of a couple of new symptoms: I was starting to itch, and some of my joints were starting to ache quite badly.

"It's OK," I told myself. "Just hang on and you'll be home soon. Everything will be OK then."

I couldn't have been more wrong.

Chapter 15

Fearing the Lord

A FEW YEARS BACK, I SAT in meetings at the world church headquarters with some of the other spouses of church administrators. My energy was low that day and the smile on my face probably owed more to determination than anything else.

The main speaker for the morning session was an energetic, talented lady who spoke at length about making the most of one's role as the spouse of a pastor. She described the many projects she coordinated and the initiatives she'd begun which complemented her husband's ministry.

I came home that afternoon feeling terribly inadequate. No matter who we are, or what public persona we project, I suspect at times we all sometimes feel confronted by a sense of our own limitations. Through the years, I've usually done a reasonable job of keeping these feelings in perspective. Yet, today my contributions to the Lord's cause felt rather pitiful.

Later that evening, I opened my Bible. At the time I was reading through some passages in Psalms and I came to a few lines in Psalm 147 that stopped me in my tracks. I read:

> "His pleasure is not in the strength of the horse,
> nor his delight in the legs of the warrior;
> the LORD delights in those who fear him,
> who put their hope in his unfailing love"
>   (Psalm 147:10, 11, NIV).

Since that day, I've kept a copy of these words on a slip of paper in the back of my Bible. It reminds me that one of the hardest parts of being a Christian is grasping the fact that it's *God's* strength, not ours, that really counts.

In our humanness, we say to God, "Look what I can give You, Lord!" And He says, "It's really not about your gifts; what matters is that you accept *My* gift of grace."

How radically our perspective can be changed by this simple, yet hard-to-absorb fact. Suddenly, we don't need to use our "spiritual output" as a measuring stick for self-worth. The God we serve takes pleasure, instead, when we recognize our own weakness and place our "hope in his unfailing love."

For me, there are a number of very practical, everyday principles that flow from this reality.

First, I've found that there's never any benefit in playing the "I wish" game. "I wish things had been different"; "I wish I had the ability to do this or that"; "I wish that such and such had never happened to me." I've found that it's far healthier in any situation to say, instead, "Well, this is who I am, and these are the circumstances in which I find myself. So, what am I going to do with what I have?"

Second, comparing ourselves to other people is always a losing proposition. It's the fastest route I know to dissatisfaction and unhappiness.

Third, and for me, this is perhaps the most important point: *We have to learn to "cut the garment to suit the cloth."* This old English proverb has come back to me through the years in many different situations and it never fails to clear away some of the fog that may have clouded my thinking. You can't make a suit out of a piece of scrap fabric; you've simply got to work with what you have. With God's help, though, you can still make something beautiful.

Worse than heroin

I sat on a leather sofa in the living room of our home in St. Albans, England. My eyes were fixed on the face of a clock that sat on the windowsill across the room from me.

"Only twenty seconds to go," I said to myself. "Ten seconds. Only five seconds. I made it. Now, let's start again. Fifty seconds. Forty seconds. I'm almost halfway there. Thirty seconds. Twenty seconds. . . ."

The clock hands moved with glacial speed. Each tick was maddeningly deliberate. Precise. The clock was my persecutor and my savior. Its hands marked off the seconds, minutes, and hours of an all-enveloping agony that had taken up residence in my body. As I counted off the minutes, I mined my memory for every good book I'd read, beautiful music I'd heard, every happy moment our family had shared.

I've been told since then that withdrawal from steroids can be worse than withdrawal from heroin addiction. I don't doubt it.

I'd left the National Institutes of Health in Washington, D.C., a few days earlier against the advice of the doctors there—they knew what withdrawal could entail and they were sure that without constant support, I would start increasing my steroid dose again.

Jan had met my plane in London, but by this time the niggling itching and aching I'd noticed before take-off in Washington had intensified into something alarming. I was determined, though, not to let Jan know the extent of my pain—I knew he'd insist on canceling his trip to the United States.

After he left the following day, I spent my days propped on the sofa, watching the clock. The aching was of a type I've never experienced before or since, and it covered my entire body. Even the tips of my teeth seemed to throb. I've never been so close to losing my mind; it was indescribable. I had thought myself well-acquainted with pain, but this was another thing altogether

Later, I described to my doctor at the NIH the survival technique I'd come up with; how I'd divided the hours into fifteen-minute blocks of agony, willing myself to hold on from one minute to the next.

"Kari," he said, "when you left the hospital to go home to England, no one here expected you to endure the withdrawal on your own—we were sure you'd be back or that you'd simply give in and increase your steroid dose."

"Well," I said. "I'm stubborn."

At the time, though, even my stubborn nature was taxed to the limit. Sleep became elusive. When Jan phoned from Washington, where he was attending Annual Council at the church headquarters, I willed myself not to let on what was happening.

Three days before Jan was due to come home, I broke down on the phone one evening and told him.

He was furious—not with me, but with the doctors at the NIH. He immediately drove from Takoma Park to Bethesda and confronted my lead doctor.

"What have you done to my wife?" he said. "She's in hell over there."

The doctor explained the need to drop my steroid dose to an appropriate level, and the consequences of the withdrawal process.

"How long will it last?" asked Jan.

"Perhaps three months at this intensity," said the doctor, "but some of the symptoms will be with her for up to three years."

I was so thankful to see Jan walking through the door. He could wash me, dress me, and care for me and my relief was profound.

The first sign that the pain would eventually let up came a couple of weeks later, when one day I noticed that some of my teeth had stopped aching. Then, as the days went by, some of my joints began to feel just a bit less painful.

Residual pain continued on and off for the next couple of years—an arthriticlike discomfort that came on especially when I was tired—but it was bearable.

New directions

Adjusting to my new treatment plan under the care of the NIH may have been a prolonged and painful business, but there were a couple of unexpected silver linings.

First, in a roundabout way, my experience led me to a new field of interest—psychology. While receiving inpatient care at the NIH, my doctor informed me they'd arranged for me to see a psychiatrist. Taken aback, I made it clear I felt no need for any such care. In spite of my protests, I dutifully went to the appointment and took great satisfaction when, at the end of our session, the psychiatrist told me I was doing just fine and there was absolutely no need for any follow-up appointments.

I did, however, learn a startling fact: most Addison's patients suffer profound depression. In fact, many Addison sufferers are diagnosed only after being referred to an endocrinologist by their psychologist or psychiatrist.

When I returned to St. Albans and life began to feel somewhat normal again, I began to wonder why I'd largely escaped the terrible emotional trauma so common to my fellow Addison patients. This, in turn, led me to the study of psychology. The Anglican Church in England ran a network of counseling centers throughout the country and also offered a three-year course of study in psychology and counseling. I completed the course and was afterward asked to join the staff of the St. Albans Counseling Center on a part-time basis, seeing patients referred by local doctors.

As my health allowed, I was able to take on one or two clients at a time, working with people damaged by various life experiences. It wasn't always easy but I found immense satisfaction in it and always came away feeling blessed. The Lord had taught me over and over again, through so many difficult periods in my life, that I had to "cut the garment to suit the cloth" and that He would care for the rest. This sense of assurance was something I longed to share with these fragile human beings who were struggling with the many difficult things life had thrown their way.

Grace

The second "silver lining" of my experience with the NIH was a profound reminder of the power and tenacity of God's grace. Throughout my life I've been taken by surprise, time and again, by grace. When I've least expected it, I've experienced shining moments of divine mercy that have become turning points in my life. As a young girl, with a life-threatening condition and a dismal home life, I nevertheless felt the call of God's Spirit, and vowed to "become a Christian" no matter what. As a teenager, I stumbled across a small group of Seventh-day Adventist group of believers who fed my soul in ways that have sustained me throughout my life, grounding me in a sense of God's love and the certainty of Christ's soon return. As a young woman in Africa, I learned to depend more fully on God even as I encountered, close up, the realities of poverty and the cruelty of war. And then later, I believe it was ultimately God's grace that pulled me through some otherwise unendurable moments in my struggle with Addison's disease.

I love Ellen White's description of God's grace, for it describes perfectly my own experience. She writes, "We did not seek after it, but *it was sent in search of us.* God rejoices to bestow this grace upon every one who hungers for it. To every one He presents terms of mercy, *not because we are worthy, but because we are so utterly unworthy. Our need is the qualification . . .*"*

Consider this for a moment. God's grace is an active force—something that is "sent in search of us." What an incredible thought! And even more—we're qualified to receive this gift simply because we need it. Our very unworthiness is what makes us "eligible" for God's mercy.

If you have trouble getting your mind around the magnitude of such a gift, then you're not alone. I've experienced God's grace so many times, and yet I still can't fully comprehend it. It is simply unfathomable that the God of the universe actively seeks us out, in all our unworthiness and messiness, and offers us something—for free—that we could never otherwise hope to obtain.

In the closing chapter of my own father's life, I again saw the mystery of God's grace at work. In 1975, the Adventist Church held its General Conference Session in Vienna, Austria—the first time a world church meeting of this type had been held outside the United States. Jan attended as a delegate and I went with him, along with our youngest son, Rein Andre. It was a wonderful experience that brought back to me many memories of the 1951 Paris Youth Congress I'd attended as a new believer. There was singing that seemed

---

* Ellen G. White, *God's Amazing Grace* (Hagerstown: Review and Herald® Publishing Association, 1973), 10; emphasis supplied.

to lift the roof; the feeling of kinship with people from so many different places; the shared sense of urgency to take God's truth "into all the world."

But just a few days into the session, I received a phone call from my mother in Norway. My father, who'd long been a heavy smoker, had been diagnosed with lung cancer and the disease was already well advanced. There was nothing to be done and my father wanted to leave the hospital and spend his last days at home. Would I be willing to come back for a time and help care for him?

I flew back to Oslo assailed by unhappy memories. With the perspective of adulthood, I knew my father's life had not been easy. He'd struggled with circumstances that had embittered him, and which had drawn out much of the joy from his life. It was not surprising, then, that he'd made our home an unhappy place. Separately, my mother and father were good people. Together, they were miserable and my siblings and I bore the scars of their unhappiness.

That summer was an unusually hot, dry one for Norway, and the well at my parents' home had dried up. The stifling days, unbroken by cooling breezes, made my father especially uncomfortable. He tossed and turned and perspired and we sponged his body down continually, trying to give him some relief. My mother sat up with him at night, while I took the day shift and we did our best to make him comfortable. But often during the night, my father grew frightened and my mother would wake me. I'd sit by his bed, hold his hand, and pray aloud.

At the end of the summer I had to return home. My Addison's had given me no respite, and the lack of sleep had taken its toll on my health. A few weeks later, my father died. I couldn't travel, but Jan flew from England to attend the funeral service.

In the last days of his life, my father—against all odds—had found peace in Christ. He had asked to be baptized into the Adventist Church, but by that stage he was far too ill. Instead, he celebrated Communion from his sickbed.

I don't know exactly what happened between my father and the Lord, but I know with certainty that God's grace was "sent in search" of my father. And I know that it found him.

In the years that followed my father's death, my mother began attending the local Adventist Church each Sabbath. She never formally joined, although she faithfully paid her tithe and became a stalwart member of the Dorcas Society. Whenever Jan and I visited her, she'd often prompt Jan of an evening with, "Isn't it time for worship yet?"

I believe I'll see my mother and father again in God's kingdom. I'm profoundly thankful that our Lord knows where each of us comes from. He knows the struggles we've faced and the circumstances that have buffeted us and helped determine our paths in life. He searches for us wherever we are, and He extends mercy and understanding that, by any external measure, we don't deserve.

Divine timing

If God has given me many lessons in the power of His grace, He's also given me many opportunities to learn about "divine timing." By nature, I have little patience with delays and sometimes I have trouble remembering that God's schedule doesn't necessarily correspond with mine. Accepting God's timing in our lives can be tremendously difficult. When we're praying for a loved one who's struggling, or a relationship that's in trouble, or a health issue, or a problem at work, we want God's intervention—or at least, His answer—*now*, not sometime down the track.

In 1 Peter, the apostle writes to a group of believers that's facing the very real threat of persecution. They're living and worshiping with the knowledge that their faith in Christ is potentially a sentence of death. To these beleaguered new Christians, Peter writes: "Humble yourselves, therefore, under God's mighty hand, that he may lift you up *in due time*. Cast all your anxiety on him because he cares for you" (1 Peter 5:6, 7, NIV).

For me, the caveat "in due time" is perhaps the most difficult part of this text and through the years of my phone ministry, I've talked with many other people who've also struggled with this. Yes, we can "humble ourselves"—acknowledge God's sovereignty in our life—and hand over our fears and hopes to Him. But then we have to be prepared to *wait.* And to trust that God will "lift us up in due time"—in *His* time.

It has taken some time, but I've come to see that waiting on God is often part of a "seasoning" process that He, in His wisdom, sometimes allows us to experience. As I look back on Jan's and my life together, I can see that events—both positive and negative—have tended to unfold in ways that have shaped and prepared us for what was to come next. At the time, it seemed that we were taking a lot of detours here and there. But in hindsight, I can see that God had a plan and was waiting for the right time—His time—to disclose it.

GC Session

In 1995, Jan and I attended another world church session, this time being held in Utrecht, the Netherlands. When the nominating committee produced its choices for new world church vice presidents, Jan's name was on the list. Some years earlier, the then-president of the General Conference had spoken to Jan about a possible vice presidential role, but after much prayer we felt the time was not right. Now, in Utrecht, faced with a decision to make, we again took it to the Lord and this time we felt we had no excuses.

It meant yet another international move. So far I'd lived in eight different countries in my quest to follow the Lord "through a land not sown." Our most recent move, from Newbold College to the division office in St. Albans, had not been far in terms of miles, but it had been a very difficult move for me. Yet after a time I'd discovered the blessings of a busy phone ministry and, eventually, the satisfaction of working as a counselor.

And now it seemed the Lord was asking me to leave behind this settled, fulfilling life and to once more head into new territory.

But it was not entirely new. In a way, it seemed the Lord was calling us full circle, back to the place where our adventure in ministry had really begun.

Having previously lived near the General Conference, I thought I knew the area well, but I was in for a surprise. The Washington, D.C., we'd experienced in the 1950s was very different to what we encountered in 1995. Where there used to be meadows and rolling hills there were now roads, houses, and more roads. Everything seemed strange and turned around, almost as if the east had turned into west. And then there was the new General Conference building itself. It was nothing like the small building we had known in Takoma Park. The new facility in Silver Spring was large and felt, at least to me, not very personal. Everyone seemed preoccupied with work, and the many friends we'd once had in the area from our student days were long gone.

Jan immediately embarked on a busy travel schedule. Since I couldn't work, I found myself spending a lot of time alone, and I sometimes felt like a very small pea in a big pod. When I began to feel sorry for myself, I took to saying, tongue-in-check, "Kari, you've got yourself for company. Aren't you lucky! Imagine all the people who'd love that!" I doubt there are too many people who'd actually feel that way about my company, but saying it always made me smile.

Slowly, after a few weeks of exploring and beginning to make new friendships, the area started to make sense to me again and I found that east was east, and west was west. My phone ministry and other rewarding tasks again began to fill my days. I was reminded once again that the most reliable way to measure the importance of what we do and how we fill our time is not to keep comparing ourselves to other people, but to simply ask, "Have I made the most of what's on *my* plate?"

I did miss Jan a lot; he spent more time traveling than he did at home. But then I'd remember my childhood where my parents, who rarely spent any time apart, produced a home filled with quarrels and discontent. I kept reminding myself that, in the end, it's not about how much time we spend with our spouse, but the quality of the time we have together; a few happy hours are worth more than a month of unhappiness. Once more, I felt blessed.

The Lord leads

Sometimes people have asked me whether "politics" happen at

the world church headquarters. I'm often tempted to reply, "Well, if you're asking me if flawed humans work at the General Conference, then the answer is obviously 'Yes.' "

Does it sometimes matter too much who you know, or what your Adventist "pedigree" is? Perhaps. Do church workers always make the right choices, or always manage to distinguish between their own desires and their duty to the Lord? Of course not. We're not in the new earth yet.

But ask me, instead, if I've seen evidence that the Lord is leading His church, or if I believe the Holy Spirit is working powerfully today in so many parts of the world field. My answer, then, is an unequivocal "Yes!"

God has no choice but to work through frail and flawed humans. Look at so many of the characters in the Old Testament. Even in the New Testament, the apostle Paul was not exactly without rough edges.

Sometimes, though, I think God's patience with His created beings must be sorely tried.

In early 1999, there came a crisis at the world church headquarters that ultimately resulted in the church's executive committee convening to choose a new church president.

On March 1, I'd just come back from a trip to England and I was in the kitchen folding clean laundry. At around six that evening, Jan arrived home from the office and came into where I was working. I knew the executive committee had met that day, and so I asked, "Do we have a new president?"

Jan sat down on a chair, and said, "Yes, the 'brethren' have chosen a new president."

"Well, is it 'so-and-so,' " I asked?

"No, it isn't him," replied Jan.

"Then who?" I asked.

"Kari, I'm afraid they've asked me," he said.

I was utterly taken aback. General Conference president! Who could measure up to that enormous task? What qualifications did we have? In our own right, none.

146

Fearing the Lord

I'd always assumed my chronic illness had given Jan an "exemption certificate." The wife of a General Conference president, I knew, had all manner of different responsibilities and opportunities, and I recognized full well that my Addison's disease would be an ever-present challenge for both of us.

I don't understand this, Lord, I thought.

Suddenly, my thoughts went into replay mode. I was seven years old again and hearing the other children say, "You're going to die." I felt scared even though I didn't really know what dying meant.

Then, I was eleven years old, lying in a hospital bed with pains too awful to describe. "If you let me live, I'll become a Christian," I had vowed to "Someone up there."

Then, I saw again that group of Seventh-day Adventist believers who met each Sabbath in a Norwegian village, their "church" a cramped living room and kitchen in a widow's house. I heard their voices singing, "Lift up the trumpet and loud let it ring" to the accompaniment of a single guitar. I felt again the tremendous sense of security and peace that came from worshiping with these simple men and women who loved the Lord, who could recite long passages from the Bible and Ellen White, and who saved all year so they could give a week's salary to the annual sacrifice offering.

Then, in my mind I traced our family's steps through the United States, Africa, Germany, and England, through episodes of both discouragement and joy. And through it all I could see the constant presence of the Lord, leading, teaching, comforting, and sustaining us at every point along our improbable journey from rural Norway to this global field to which He'd called us.

In this new chapter of our lives, I knew I couldn't offer God anything beyond the abilities and strength He had given me. I'd have to "cut the garment to fit the cloth." I couldn't make a ball gown out of just a few yards of fabric. But I could make the most of what I had. And suddenly, I felt this was all right.

Postscript

IN MANY WAYS, THE ELEVEN years from 1999 to 2010 when Jan was president of the General Conference were tremendously exciting. What an incredible privilege it was to get to know the church around the world. There's not enough space in this book to describe what the Lord did for and through His church during these years. So much could be said, but this belongs more to Jan's story than to mine. There were challenges, of course—often significant ones. But at the same time it was impossible not to feel that God was in control and that His Spirit was moving in the lives of church members we visited everywhere from Australia, to Brazil, to Russia.

There were so many wonderful people we met. Sometimes, we'd visit a church and someone would come up afterward and say, "You don't know me, but I pray for you by name every day."

The Lord must have realized we needed those prayers.

In recent years, I've had more time to reflect back on the unlikely path my life has taken. In retelling a little of my life's story, I wanted to communicate, first and foremost, my gratitude to the Lord. On the basis of where and when I was born, who my parents were, and my early years without any spiritual connection at all, I simply shouldn't be where I am today. Really, I probably ought not to be even alive. In hindsight, it seems like an absurdly tenuous chain of coincidences that led me, as a child, to the medical care I needed to fix my damaged heart. But these "coincidences" have given me almost seven decades and counting of "extra grace."

Each one of us has a personal narrative of the good and ill that has shaped our life, and the lessons we've learned along the way. For those who may be struggling with various challenges life has thrown your way, I hope my story gives you some encouragement. I hope I've been able to communicate the depth of my conviction that each one of us can fulfill God's plan for our life with the "toolbox" of talents and strengths we've been given. And so there's no need to waste energy wishing we could fundamentally change ourselves or our circumstances.

But then, having accepted who we are and whatever limitations we have, it's up to us to "cut the garment to fit the cloth." To do everything in our power to transform whatever scraps of fabric we have on hand into something beautiful. To use the strengths we *do* have to their fullest extent. And then, to be content.

Sometimes I think of this in terms of painting a picture. Perhaps the canvas we've been given to work with seems unfairly small. But whatever size it is, we can make our little painting the most beautiful we possibly can. It's never going to be a vast canvas hanging on a gallery wall. But still, it'll be the best we can do and that has immense value.

The most important thing to remember is that as we each work on our "scraps of cloth" or our "little painting," the Lord is ever-present. He's with us whether we're conscious of it or not. In His unfathomable kindness, He gives us the strength we need and He weighs our mistakes and weaknesses not using anything like my old kitchen scales, but in the scales of His eternal grace.

I've often reflected on the words of the psalmist:

Lord, you [have assigned me] my portion and my cup;
  you make my lot secure.
The boundary lines have fallen for me in pleasant places;
  surely I have a delightful inheritance (Psalm 16:5, 6, NIV).

Sometimes I did feel dissatisfied with my assigned "portion and cup." Looking back, though, I realize that my portion was more than sufficient for the purpose the Lord had in mind for me. And in the end, my "boundary lines have fallen for me in pleasant places; surely I have a delightful inheritance."

What now?

In the meantime, we're still here. Jan and I are what one might call "retired," but our days have not changed all that much. Everything is just on a smaller scale. We continue to write and to travel, as before, for various appointments, for pleasure, or to see family and friends.

At the beginning of September 2014, we went back to Vejlefjord, Denmark, to celebrate the sixtieth anniversary of our graduation from what was then the junior college for the West Nordic Union (Denmark and Norway). It brought back so many memories of May 11, 1954, the day Jan and I graduated from *"Predikantholdet,"* or the preachers' class. We had studied Greek, biblical studies, church history, and homiletics with the single goal of equipping ourselves to join "God's workforce." Our class chose as its graduation motto *"Frelst for at Tjene,"* or "Saved to Serve."

Back then, these few words summed up our life's purpose, and they still do today. So, for as long as we're down on this earth, our work will go on.

* * *

I can't finish this book without paying tribute to our three children: Laila, Jan Rune, and Rein Andre. They never had the privilege of growing up in Norway, the country of their passport. They just came along with us wherever we moved from country to country. They had to change friends, schools, and languages all too frequently, but they did so with a grace and skill that amazed us. We are tremendously proud of them.

In particular, we're proud of our eldest son, Jan Rune, and how far he has come since his near-fatal accident fourteen years ago. In 2000, he was erecting the staging and lighting for a digital television exhibition in Germany and fell some thirty feet from scaffolding onto a cement floor, sustaining terrible injuries. The story of what has happened since would fill a whole new book and more. In the years that have followed, Jan Rune has traveled a tremendously difficult path. With the support of the Lord, the love of his family, and his own incredible perseverance and hard work, he has made much progress toward recovery, but it has stopped short of being complete.

A transforming hope

I'd also like to pay tribute to the countless other children around the world who, for one reason or another, are without a country of belonging. They've been hurt by the world. They've never had the chance to form those all-important roots of family, culture, religion, or country. They often feel like they belong nowhere but have to live "everywhere." Their country of belonging remains a utopia—a place in their dreams, but nowhere to be found.

When I think of these children, I hear in my mind the sad, haunting tune of the Negro spiritual:

*"Sometimes I feel like a motherless child
A long ways from home."*

For those in our world who are suffering from a deficit of hope, we have something tangible to offer—a hope that knows no limits of past injustice, hurts, or alienation.

It's a transforming and renewing hope, expressed by the words of John the revelator. John, confined on his island prison by "walls" of ocean, wrote of a new era where "there was no longer any sea" (Revelation 21:1, NIV). Today, our prison walls—our seas—are sadness and separation, mistakes and guilt, sickness and death. But John assures us the time is coming soon when this sea of grief will be gone, and God Himself will wipe away our tears (verse 4). The promise is sweet: "I am making everything new!" (verse 5, NIV).

Then, our garment, our cloth, will be both beautiful and perfect. Amen. Come, Lord Jesus (Revelation 22:20).

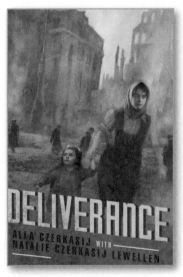
 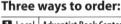